MAR 2 4 2008

San Anselmo Public Library
110 Tunstead Avenue
San Anselmo, CA 94960

DATE DUE

APR 1 7 2008

DISCARDED

DEMCO INC. 38-2931

California
Trip

POINT REYES HEADLANDS
Marin

California
Trip

Richard P. Blair
Kathleen P. Goodwin
Authors

Richard P. Blair
Photography and book design

Kathleen P. Goodwin
Additional photography

COLOR & LIGHT EDITIONS
Inverness, California

Copyright © 2008 by Color & Light Editions

Photographs and text © 2008 by

Richard Blair and Kathleen Goodwin

Book design by Richard Blair

All rights reserved. No part of this book may be re-
produced in any form or by any electronic means,
including information storage and retrieval systems,
without permission in writing from the publisher, except by a reviewer who may quote brief passages in a
review. Please do not illustrate from these images.

First Edition

ISBN 0-9671527-3-9

Library of Congress Card Number: 2006908602

Printed in Singapore by Craftprint

Contents

VIEW FROM THE BAY RIDGE TRAIL, SUNSET AND FOG
Point Reyes National Seashore
KATHLEEN GOODWIN

Preface

THROUGHOUT THE WORLD, CALIFORNIA IS THE ULTIMATE ADDRESS. It has come to represent a blend of fantasy and reality. With its stunning natural beauty, cities, diverse population, and powerhouse economy, the Golden State does indeed offer the promise of a better life, of dreams fulfilled.

Millions of people have flocked here over the past 150 years, chasing their dreams in a migration that continues to this day. This constant influx of new ideas and energy, combined with California's natural resources, provides the fuel that keeps the state humming.

California has a long and rambling geography: from the rain forests of the north to the extreme deserts of Death Valley, rolling hills of the coast, and the mountainous Sierra. The Central Valley and Napa Valley are wonders of agriculture. We are a world within a state.

This book is a serious look at the state from two artists who became Californians and spent decades unraveling California's mixture of natural beauty and ambitious population, economic might and wild subcultures. Over the past four years we revisited many areas to find just the photograph we needed to tell our story.

We are hoping these images will offer food for thought as California approaches the crossroads of opportunity and calamity that lies ahead. In the end, the fate of California depends on our collective willingness to manage the delicate balance among environmental, economic, and social concerns for the benefit of all.

MITZI AND CHELSEA, HOME BIRTH, 1977
Berkeley
KATHLEEN GOODWIN

SADDLE, HOME RANCH
Point Reyes

Notes from Richard Blair

TO A YOUNG MAN PEERING OUT THE WINDOW OF A SAN FRANCISCO AIRPORTER BUS, CALIFORNIA TRULY WAS THE PROMISED LAND. There was an electricity and vibrancy in the air. The colors seemed pure and saturated that spring day in 1969. I'll photograph California, showing it to be the futuristic, fantastic plastic lover that I need, I thought.

I had been photographing in NYC and had produced a body of black and white images on street life. I had also just broken up with my girlfriend. I was here to make a fresh start and to explore wild places–both in the High Sierra climbing mountains, and in some new relationships. Like many people who come to California, I was escaping, but I hoped to escape to a land where the future was limitless.

I had been to California once before, in 1967, living with the flower children in the Haight and spending a summer camping in Yosemite. That was the real attraction now: the Sierras were the perfect place to climb and backpack. Stupendous mountains, cool pure air, rushing water as pure as the sky. It was a place to get healthy and fit, and I could meet people on the trails and in the campgrounds.

My new life took some unexpected turns. I became park photographer in Yosemite in the early 70s. Later I moved to Berkeley, meeting Kathleen Goodwin in 1976 at a hippie breakfast hangout, Smokey Joe's Cafe. That year I set up a commercial photography studio. My first big clients were the Port of Oakland and Bezerkeley Records. I also learned graphic arts camerawork and platemaking for duotones and special effects. We had a monster Japanese graphic arts camera that did 2 x 3-foot film for large lithographs and silk screens!

Many years spent shooting in the studio taught me the techniques to get exactly what I wanted on film, which has proved invaluable for my work in the field as a fine art photographer. Thirty-seven years later, I look back at those early days and think that it took a long time to do this book! I had a lot to learn about California. I had to drive for a million miles to see what I have seen, and now I have completed the project that I started as a twenty-year-old on the bus from the airport.

The odyssey began as an exploration of the state. After hundreds of trips, Kathleen and I realized we had important knowledge about our new home, and many ideas and skills to share with readers.

We felt that California picture books had not gone deep enough–that pictures of beaches and tourist attractions were not enough, that they were missing the real issues and many of the amazing things that California is known for. Where was high tech and DNA? Where were the gay Californians, and what about the big issues–immigration for one? Friends suggested other subjects such as the huge population of inmates in our prisons, and since pot is said to be our biggest cash crop, where was *that*?

Another element was our politics and our style. We were radicals, not Republicans! We had a point of view that was missing from the other books, which seemed whitewashed by publishers afraid to be outspoken.

California is a harbinger of the future, one of the most influential places in myriad ways. It is a ridiculously complex subject, and we went to work filling in gaps in our travels and getting the subject matter necessary to present as complete a book as possible. Over the past four years we traveled to specific regions to complete our overview of the entire state. The result was 600 pages of finished text and images; hence this is the first of a series. We wish we could have included more, but 300 pages and 600 images is a practical limit.

Some of the photographs involved shooting quickly–before the police showed up near Harris Ranch, for example, called by a security guard. Other images were the result of being at the right place and time. The ultra-long time frame of more than 30 years in collecting images for this book helped enormously, along with those coincidences that lead to great photographs.

It has been said that California has a fatal beauty, that its charms attract too many people and there are too many exploiters preying on its resources. Some of the images in *California Trip* are necessarily critical, but important for the public to see.

It's a thorny problem for an artist, to create a book that inspires and educates rather than a tome that might get critical acclaim but not influence people as I hope to do with *California Trip*.

I have always thought that an important function of photography is social and political critique. These pages are the result of that belief. They are also an attempt to show another generation the way forward. I hope they, too, go on the road, Kerouac-style, exploring California, relishing the freedom of being nowhere in particular but the right spot nevertheless.

Hang on for the ride and enjoy the book!

–Richard Blair

Inverness, California

1969 *2007*

KAYAKER AT DAWN, WHITE HOUSE POOL
Point Reyes
KATHLEEN GOODWIN

Notes from Kathleen Goodwin

I AM ONE OF THOSE THOUSANDS OF IMMIGRANTS SOME PEOPLE ARE SO CONCERNED ABOUT.

California has been my adopted home since 1974. I came here because it was a free society, unlike my native South Africa. After getting a university degree in mathematics and chemistry I gravitated to newspaper journalism. My country was still embroiled in a racist apartheid regime, so I embraced and still celebrate California's tolerance and innovation.

Arriving without a working visa, I became a street artist, making and selling feather jewelry at fairs and on Telegraph Avenue in Berkeley. This was the practical equivalent of a getting a business degree... fast!

In 1976 I met Richard and we married in 1978. During the eighties and nineties we had a photography studio in Berkeley, which produced book, magazine and album covers, and did work for many innovative designers in the bay area. After the success of our first book, *Point Reyes Visions*, which was published soon after we moved to Inverness, we dropped commercial photography and became self-supporting artists, writers and publishers. Our work is widely collected and to a large extent supports us.

By the late 1970s I decided to pursue painting seriously and studied at San Francisco State University. Painting is still my first love.

Photography has always been a big part of our travels. I have adapted to using cameras, first for recording scenes for visual remembrances, then realizing that sometimes the images were best as photographs themselves, I became skilled at printing them in the studio. So now I am a photographer as well as a painter and I show both mediums in galleries. With the advances in digital print making I use large-format printers both to print photographic images and to make prints of my paintings in editions.

The miles traveled researching this book have been unfailingly interesting. Around each corner another quirky piece of California presented itself. The odyssey did not start as a research project but as an exploration of the state.

Our books hark back to another age. In the earliest days of bookmaking, artisans controlled the production of an entire book: writing the text, creating illustrations, designing the cover, and printing the final result. Books were very much hand-made. Technology and the development of mass production brought radical changes, diluting the art of bookmaking to the point where these days, the artist who illustrates a book cover has rarely even read the text.

With the invention of computers and scanners, the tide has once again turned. The control of a book can return to one person or, in our case, two. We control all phases of production, from taking the photographs and writing the text to designing and numbering each page. We design each page individually until it pleases us. There is no rule to follow, only that of balance, beauty and appropriate choice of images. We stand next to the printer at the press to ensure the final stage is to our liking. We even drive to bookstores with our books in hand! This way of working is the fruition of a philosophy of independence we conceived of in the 60s and that we never forgot.

I have now come full circle—writing about California's problems and opportunities as I once did about my home country as a journalist in South Africa. Making this book has profoundly deepened my understanding and appreciation of California and its people.

–Kathleen Goodwin
Inverness, California

1976

Teakettle Junction, Death Valley, 2006

Chapter 1

Big Sur Coast

...this poor haunted canyon which again gives me the willies as we walk under the bridge and come to those heartless breakers busting in on sand higher than earth and looking like the heartlessness of wisdom.

–Jack Kerouac, Big Sur 1962

Classic Seaside Cottage
Whaler's Cove, Point Lobo

Adult Brown Pelican
Monterey Bay

This bird is in breeding plumage. Pelicans have made a great recovery from near extinction. DDT, the pesticide, was making their eggshells too thin, so the eggs would break rather that hatch. Since DDT was banned in 1972, the birds have rebounded wonderfully.

SURF, ROCKS, MOUNTAINS
Rocky Point

BIXBY BRIDGE

ARTICHOKE FARM

On my first trip up Highway One, I was in a VW that could only go 30 miles an hour. I had a slow drive punctuated with frequent stops as we allowed vehicles by. It was a very good introduction!

DEETJEN'S BIG SUR INN
Castro Creek

COVE
Point Lobos

ROCK INLET
Point Lobos

THE JAMES HOUSE
Carmel Highlands

This is the famous Greene and Greene *James House* built out of native granite rock south of Carmel. The Greene brothers were pioneers of the Arts and Crafts Movement. One can see their work in Pasadena, notably at the *Gamble House*. A few, very fortunate people have migrated out of Carmel and built their own Shangri-las on cliff edges.

Now the era of developing California's coast is coming to an end. The land is protected by the Coastal Commission and local activists.

COTTAGE VIEW
Lucia

Fog and Hills
Nacimiento - Fergusson Road

Male Elephant Seal

Whale Skull

Vulture Drying Its Wings

Wave, Point Lobos

MANUEL PEAK (ELEV. 3,520)

Rare is the person who is not stunned by the sight of successive rocky cliffs plunging into the Pacific Ocean.

PICO BLANCO (ELEV. 3,455)

TIMBER TOP (ELEV. 3,120)

JULIA PFEIFFER BURNS STATE PARK IS ONE OF THE GEMS OF BIG SUR. The park stretches from the Big Sur coastline into nearby 3,000-foot ridges. It features redwood, tan oak, madrone, chaparral, and an 80-foot waterfall that drops from granite cliffs into the ocean from the Overlook Trail.

Sadly, the park was unable the stop the highway department from dumping dirt into the cove that contains McWay Falls, a beautiful waterfall that used to fall directly into the sea at high tide. Now a beach is at its base. It is still beautiful.

There is a bench at the end of the Overlook Trail that is a perfect place to watch for gray whales migrating southward in December and January and returning north in March and April. If you are extraordinarily lucky, you might see a whale in the cove. Sea otters, harbor seals and California sea lions are a more common sight. Black cormorants, seagulls, brown pelicans and black oystercatchers are frequently observed here.

McWay Falls From Sea Level
In my youth I climbed down the very rough path.
This view is now off-limits.

McWay Falls (pre-1983)
Julia Pfeiffer Burns State Park

McWay Falls (post-1983)
Julia Pfeiffer Burns State Park

Soberanes Point
Big Sur Coast

11

Chapter 2

The North Coast

Wander a whole summer if you can... the time will not be taken from the sum of life.

–John Muir

A Stream Returns to the Sea
Mendocino Coast

The *Sunshine* on Drakes Beach

THE WRECK OF THE SUNSHINE

When the storms hit California in the winter, the winds and waves come from the south. If the anchorage is open to the fury of the storm, a boat can drag its anchor or break the anchor chain or rode. The sailors on the *Sunshine* took refuge in Drakes Bay which gave them no protection because our storms come from the south. They tried to motor off after their anchor broke, but the storm tossed the boat onto the beach at Point Reyes National Seashore. The couple were planning to travel to the Caribbean via the Panama Canal, but on their first night out the storm almost destroyed their dreams. The boat's hull cracked, but the crew survived when the *Sunshine* was thrown up on the beach. With help from a backhoe, a tractor and an experienced man who chanced upon the wreck, they were able to fix the hull and float the boat off the sand. A year later they set off once more. We wish them luck and caution them to pay close attention to the weather! California's coast can be violent, particularly in the winter. Sneaker waves—extra big waves that arrive without warning—sweep people from the shore or knock them into rocks. Never turn your back on the sea.

The Sailors Salvage the Sails

Crescent City Lighthouse

POINT ARENA LIGHTHOUSE
Gualala Area

POINT REYES HEADLANDS AND DRAKES BAY, STORMY
Point Reyes National Seashore

This grand show is eternal. It is always sunrise somewhere; the dew is never all dried at once; a
shower is forever falling; vapor ever rising. Eternal sunrise, eternal sunset, eternal dawn and gloaming,
on seas and continents and islands, each in its turn,
as the round earth rolls. –*John Muir*

FERN CANYON
Humboldt Coast

GREAT BEACH AT SUNSET
Point Reyes National Seashore
KATHLEEN GOODWIN

WILDERNESS COAST
Point Reyes National Seashore

SAILBOAT ON DAPPLED SEA
KATHLEEN GOODWIN

DRAKES BEACH
Point Reyes National Seashore
KATHLEEN GOODWIN

WAVE AND CHIMNEY ROCK
Point Reyes National Seashore

SUN, FOG & TREE
Tomales

SEA RANCH CHAPEL

Woodworking humble to grand... Tourists buy chainsaw art, in this case from a chewing-tobacco outfitted dude.

The huge forests in Northern California inspired many generations of carpenters. They built Victorian houses with elaborate gingerbread facades out of California's once abundant redwood.

The unusual structure above is the Sea Ranch Chapel, a nondenominational chapel built near Mendocino for meditation and prayer. Designed in 1984 by James T. Hubbell, a San Diego-based artist, it was made with local stone, redwood, teak and cedar by a team of artists and craftspeople living in the community. It is open daily for all.

CHAINSAW CARVER
Humboldt

MILL CREEK
Jedediah Smith Redwoods State Park

HAULING OUT
Bolinas

JIGGING FOR EEL
Salt Point State Park

CRAB POT AND FLOATS
Bodega Harbor

BEACHED REDWOOD TREES
Humboldt Coast

HERRING FISHING IN TOMALES BAY (2)

MONTEREY STYLE FISHING BOATS
Tomales Bay

SALMON BOATS, OUTGOING TIDE
Bolinas Lagoon

COBRA LILY FLOWER
KATHLEEN GOODWIN

COBRA LILIES
Darlingtonia Trail

THE SMITH RIVER
Northern Humboldt County
The Smith River is unique since it is the only
river system without any dam in California.

CALIFORNIA'S OWN FLESH-EATING PLANT

The Cobra Lily, *Darlingtonia Californica*, is a rare carnivorous plant in Northern California. The name comes from its tubular leaves' similarity to a rearing cobra, complete with a forked leaf—ranging from yellow to purplish-green—that resembles "fangs" or a serpent's "tongue." It lures insects with a sweet nectar inside the leaf opening under its hood.

Once inside, the insect becomes confused by the multiple transparent areas of the upper leaf surfaces, which appear to be exits. As the insect checks these false exits searching for an escape route, it is led down the tube structure and is unable to return to the top of the plant because of the slippery smooth surface of the inner tube and the sharp, downward pointing hairs. Eventually the insect falls into a pool of liquid. Colonies of the Cobra Lily are found mostly over serpentine rock rich in metals that most plants cannot tolerate. To survive in this habitat the California pitcher plant has evolved to be an insect eater to supplement its nutrition.

MALE TULE ELK
Point Reyes National Seashore

WILD IRIS
Humboldt

DAIRY BARN AND INVERNESS RIDGE
Marin

WATER TOWER
Mendocino

REDWOODS AND RHODODENDRONS
Mendocino   27

Chapter 3

Yosemite Valley and the High Sierra

Yosemite Valley, to me, is always a sunrise, a glitter of green and golden wonder in a vast edifice of stone and space.

—Ansel Adams

Half Dome from the Diving Board

ROCK CLIMBER RAPPELLING
Lower Yosemite Falls

BRIDALVEIL FALLS
WITH FROZEN
SPRAY

31

AN INTRODUCTION TO JOHN MUIR'S WRITING

John Muir is one of America's greatest nature writers. He had numerous adventures, including the first ascents of many peaks, and he even rode an avalanche (see his description, next page). Once he climbed behind Yosemite Falls and watched the moonlight through the falling water by wedging himself between an ice block and the cliff. Not only was he a wild poet of nature, he was also a careful observer, a botanist, and a geologist who discerned the patterns of glacial movements in the polish of the rocks and the shapes of the peaks. His writing inspired the creation of the National Park System.

RIDING A TREE

I made choice of the tallest of a group of Douglas Spruces that were growing close together like a tuft of grass, no one of which seemed likely to fall unless all the rest fell with it. Though comparatively young, they were about 100 feet high, and their lithe, brushy tops were rocking and swirling in wild ecstasy. Being accustomed to climb trees in making botanical studies, I experienced no difficulty in reaching the top of this one, and never before did I enjoy so noble an exhilaration of motion. The slender tops fairly flapped and swished in the passionate torrent, bending and swirling backward and forward, round and round, tracing indescribable combinations of vertical and horizontal curves, while I clung with muscles firm braced, like a bobo-link on a reed.

In its widest sweeps my tree-top described an arc of from twenty to thirty degrees, but I felt sure of its elastic temper, having seen others of the same species still more severely tried—bent almost to the ground indeed, in heavy snows—without breaking a fiber. I was therefore safe, and free to take the wind into my pulses and enjoy the excited forest from my superb outlook. The view from here must be extremely beautiful in any weather. Now my eye roved over the piny hills and dales as over fields of waving grain, and felt the light running in ripples and broad swelling undulations across the valleys from ridge to ridge, as the shining foliage was stirred by corresponding waves of air. Oftentimes these waves of reflected light would break up suddenly into a kind of beaten foam, and again, after chasing one another in regular order, they would seem to bend forward in concentric curves, and disappear on some hillside, like sea-waves on a shelving shore. The quantity of light reflected from the bent needles was so great as to make whole groves appear as if covered with snow, while the black shadows beneath the trees greatly enhanced the effect of the silvery splendor.

– From *The Mountains of California*, 1894

Few Yosemite visitors ever see snow avalanches and fewer still know the exhilaration of riding on them. In all my mountaineering I have enjoyed only one avalanche ride, and the start was so sudden and the end came so soon I had but little time to think of the danger that attends this sort of travel, though at such times one thinks fast. One fine Yosemite morning after a heavy snowfall, being eager to see as many avalanches as possible and wide views of the forest and summit peaks in their new white robes before the sunshine had time to change them, I set out early to climb by a side cañon to the top of a commanding ridge a little over three thousand feet above the Valley. On account of the looseness of the snow that blocked the cañon I knew the climb would require a long time, some three or four hours as I estimated; but it proved far more difficult than I had anticipated. Most of the way I sank waist deep, almost out of sight in some places. After spending the whole day to within half an hour or so of sundown, I was still several hundred feet below the summit. Then my hopes were reduced to getting up in time to see the sunset. But I was not to get summit views of any sort that day, for deep trampling near the cañon head, where the snow was strained, started an avalanche, and I was swished down to the foot of the cañon as if by enchantment. The wallowing ascent had taken nearly all day, the descent only about a minute. When the avalanche started I threw myself on my back and spread my arms to try to keep from sinking. Fortunately, though the grade of the cañon is very steep, it is not interrupted by precipices large enough to cause outbounding or free plunging. On no part of the rush was I buried. I was only moderately imbedded on the surface or at times a little below it, and covered with a veil of back-streaming dust particles; and as the whole mass beneath and about me joined in the flight there was no friction, though I was tossed here and there and lurched from side to side. When the avalanche swedged and came to rest I found myself on top of the crumpled pile without bruise or scar.

–From *The Yosemite*, 1912

Merced River and Cathedral Rocks
Yosemite Valley Near El Capitan

HALF DOME AND
WASHINGTON COLUMN
Yosemite Valley

36

John Muir was so moved by the beauty and splendor of Yosemite that he spent much of his life trying to protect it. Now all of us must preserve the park.

The amazing granite cliffs, architectural in form, the verdant meadows, the stupendous waterfalls, the pristine Merced River—all these draw almost four million visitors a year to Yosemite.

Each visitor has to work hard to have an aesthetic experience. The secret to enjoy Yosemite Valley is to go when it is not too crowded. However, most vacations are in the summer when schools are out, and the valley can be full at any time, so here's our advice: Explore the western end of the valley, where it is not developed. Walk along the river or out into the meadow away from the cars. Bring a picnic lunch and find your own paradise. Yosemite is so magical that just sitting and observing can be awe-inspiring.

Take an early morning hike to the base of one of the many waterfalls to really appreciate and experience their wonder. A moonlit walk would almost certainly ensure solitude, and you can see moonbows, like rainbows, in the mists of the waterfalls.

The valley has extensive trails and a free shuttle bus service. There are bike paths and a bike loop, part of which, sadly, is shared with traffic. Consider taking a trail that climbs out of the valley. The views are much better above the trees. Yosemite has

Lovers, Horsetail Falls and River Mist
Merced River and El Capitan

1,400 miles of trails throughout the park.

Spring brings green meadows and flowers, particularly dogwood blossoms. The waterfalls are at their height, since the snow has been melting on the high peaks. Combinations of hot weather and spring rains can cause huge cataracts of water over the cliffs

into the river. Don't go in the water then, it's a killer. Sometimes the spring floods wash over the valley floor, renewing the meadows and sweeping away buildings! When the waterfalls are big, mosquitoes are everywhere, so bring long-sleeved clothing, repellent and bug hats.

During the summer, hikers and backpackers should head for the high country, the area of the park above 8,000 feet, to avoid the heat and crowds of Yosemite Valley. The weather is generally perfect for hiking at the higher elevations, with 70 degree temperatures the norm during the day.

There are ways to cope with the summer heat in the valley. A swim in the Merced is a thrill. Floating down the river—looking up at the domes and the cliffs—is an extraordinary experience on an air mattress, inner tube, or a small inflatable boat. Don't forget float jackets for kids and rusty swimmers.

In the fall the crowds thin and the autumn colors are wonderful. Peace returns to Yosemite. California's Indian summers are a smart time to visit the entire park and the high Sierra if one is equipped for the rare early-season storms.

When I lived in the valley I remembered waiting for the first snowstorm, which always seemed to come well after Christmas. After a few days of a fierce storm, the snow would stop falling and the air would clear.

Snow would be plastered all over the cliffs, creating beautiful landscapes, and for a few days it would be a photographer's paradise. Birds and animals would reappear and the early, brave cross-country skiers would make tracks. Eventually the roads would reopen and the park would revert to being busy again. The way to experience this winter miracle is to visit Yosemite just before a big winter storm, and stay safely put in a room or sturdy tent until after the storm clears.

Yosemite Valley was the birthplace of big-wall rock climbing; many of the most advanced routes are in the valley, particu-

UPPER YOSEMITE FALLS
Yosemite Valley

larly on El Capitan. There is always a crowd of observers with binoculars watching rock climbers on their multi-day ascents. Virtually all the world's great rock climbers have paid their dues in the valley.

There is a group of visitors, *Yosemite-addicts* I call them, who fall in love with the valley. They sometimes work as ski or rock-climbing instructors or for the park. They spend years and years in the valley mesmerized by the beauty of the cliffs. I spent many summers in Yosemite with this band of gypsies. Perhaps we all felt if we looked at the cliffs just a couple more times we would unlock some cosmic secret. Then we could read the walls like an open book.

It is a little-known fact that in 1970 there was a terrible riot in the valley between the hippies and the rangers. Kids came up to Yosemite in large numbers. They occupied campsites and stayed up late. Their parties caused confrontations with the rangers. During the day, large crowds of kids would hang out in the meadow, some smoking dope. When the rangers moved in to arrest people who felt that it was unjustified, tempers flared. The confrontations continued between increasingly larger groups of kids and rangers. This was during the height of the Vietnam War, when there was tremendous resentment of the draft and the immorality of the war. The encounters escalated until hundreds of people battled for a day and night. Rangers deputized the cowboys from the stables, who

RIOT TRAINING IN YOSEMITE, 1972

rode into crowds of kids with bullwhips and clubs. Two patrol cars were burned and scores of people were injured and arrested before the passions of all involved were extinguished.

The next year the head of the Park Service,

SLEEPING OUT IN CAMP 4

George Hartzog, came to the valley and told the Yosemite Park Service to start a youth program to defuse the situation. The Yosemite Light Brigade was formed; their job was to educate the crowds of hippies who were flocking to Yosemite to experience their brand of freedom in the Great Outdoors.

In 1971, I was appointed park photographer for the National Park Service in Yosemite National Park. My job was to portray Yosemite's new era of fewer cars. I was also part of the group of artists who made up the Yosemite Light Brigade. Equipped with a powerful sound system, we put on light shows in an isolated part of the valley called Happy Isles. Images were projected on a giant screen while psychedelic music played. The park's nature slides, including my photographs, were shown simultaneously on twenty pulsing slide projectors. We silk-screened posters to put around the valley so the kids would know where the shows were happening. We led skinny-dipping excursions up Illouette Canyon, whose isolation afforded privacy. A special youth campground was developed near the bottom of the

TOURIST SEATED NEXT TO BACKPACK

Four Mile Trail, also an isolated area. Square dances with a caller were arranged to mix the hippies and the older crowd in a friendly fashion. Due to our efforts, the riots stopped completely and a lot of kids got turned on to the national parks.

Thirty years later, a former member of the Yosemite Light Brigade and my long time friend, David Vassar, made an incredible movie, *Spirit of Yosemite*, which is shown daily at the Valley Visitor Center.

The Light Brigade, with its impetuous can-do attitude, was no match for the conservative forces of the Park Service bureaucracy. After Director Hartzog was replaced by a more conservative politician appointed by President Nixon, the group was disbanded, as flurries of memos attacked our unconventional methods of accomplishing things that did not meet strict park protocol. We had solved a huge problem for the Park Service but few could see the big picture of what we had achieved.

Unfortunately, the Park Service found it difficult to implement massive change in Yosemite because of the entrenched economic and political interests that had the park in a stranglehold of power. That the Park Service could not limit motorized transport in the valley is a tragedy. The noise and pollution from vehicles, particularly unmuffled motorcycles, is sometimes overwhelming. It completely destroys the feeling of being in a nature reserve. The traffic is also dangerous for wild animals, bicyclists and pedestrians.

The essence of the valley—the peacefulness, the freshness of the pine-scented air, the gentle sounds of the Merced River, the crashing waterfalls—these sensations are lost if the park isn't managed and respected for what it is—perhaps the most beautiful valley on earth.

Yosemite Valley has a history of entrepreneurs making hefty profits from

TOURIST TRAM

tourists. Hotels, camps and even a horse racing track were built as soon as Yosemite began attracting visitors. Later came golf courses, skating rinks, gas stations, and tennis courts. Now the valley is built up, with a shopping mall, a bank, thousands of hotel beds, many restaurants, maintenance facilities, employee homes and dormitories—all of which, taken as a whole, disgust park lovers seeking a natural experience and attract those who want their vacation to be a combination of sightseeing, shopping and resort-type fun. Yosemite is now visited by a great mass of tourists with only an incidental interest in nature.

The attraction of Yosemite as a "wonder-of-the-world" provides an opportunity for Yosemite Valley to be a learning place that

OVERCROWDING IS NO FUN
Yosemite Falls Parking Lot

educates people about the joys of nature and the need for its conservation–sort of a halfway house for people from the red states. Cool, approachable Park Service rangers could educate tourists for the better, but the Park Service in Yosemite is hot under the collar. The rangers there have always had a battle mentality when it comes to visitor services. The problem is that Yosemite Valley is a city, with city crimes, so the Park Service rangers have to step in with the heavy hand of law enforcement. There are serious crimes committed in the park, and it has a busy jail, but rangers should be trained to be level-headed, with a calm attitude toward their jobs, and they should be able to educate and inform people of the joys of the park and to teach them a secret to enjoying Yosemite–namely, getting out of their cars and turning the engines off.

Yosemite Valley has one huge influence, that of the concessionaire that operates the main tourist business in the park.

Untold millions of dollars are spent in Yosemite by visitors for services provided by Delaware North, a $1.6 billion privately owned corporation, which has more than $300 million of business in America's parks.

TRAFFIC AT YOSEMITE LODGE
Yosemite Valley

Concessionaires pressure the U.S. Congress and political appointees, always citing visitor demand. Yosemite has had a regular expansion of services since I worked there in 1972. Well-meaning park service professionals can't resist the lobbying efforts of these large businesses, who, keep in mind, are only leasing the park facilities. The tail wags the dog.

FERN SPRING
Yosemite Valley

Let's rethink this system. Couldn't nonprofits or publicly funded organizations keep things a lot more mellow? When I worked in Yosemite, if a park employee dared to publicly criticize the Yosemite Park & Curry Company, then the concessionaire, they were fired for it. After the public found out how little the Curry Company had been paying the park for its contract–less than one percent of its revenues for 93 years–people were outraged by the giveaway, which was perhaps hidden by park employees' inability to speak out.

The concessions should be run by the government or an environmental non-profit organization so the business is managed appropriately. Parks should get out of the Disneyland scenario and step back, *way back*,

to a managed resource, not a managed resort! There is a better way to preserve Yosemite, and that way begins with peace and quiet and mellowness, and scaling back services to a park-like level. The time to fight for those changes is during a sympathetic administration. The current one would privatize the parks if they could get away with it.

Here are some more ideas to improve the valley. The simplest and the best idea: park the cars out of the valley and bus the people in with quiet, non-polluting buses. Campgrounds within the valley should be walk-in, with only a few communal fire rings to keep the valley from becoming filled with smoke. The buses could have room for people's camping gear, and carts could be used to ferry stuff to the campsite.

RVs should be left in landscaped parking lots out of the valley. We should ban rental RVs with their sickening advertising. They are selling portable hotel rooms, destroying the campgrounds with overcrowding and blocking the roads with slow-moving traffic. According to our count, half the RVs in Yosemite are from two rental companies. Bus in the RVers.

A car-free valley could have improved

UGLY ADVERTISING
Olmstead Point, Yosemite High Country

access for the disabled so they can see the valley too. Maybe with electric golf carts.

Support from corporations should be acknowledged with a small plaque in the Visitors Center, not with signs out in the meadows and woods. Let's separate philanthropy from advertising!

More ranger-educators (called interpreters) should be hired. If Yosemite has one great gift for humanity, it is the ability to heal, to spread peace, and to teach people a love of the planet. In the 1970s there were more than fifty seasonal rangers presenting interpretive programs, paid out of the park budget. Now, because of budget cuts, there are four! The salaries of just a few more come from what the U.S. Government calls "soft money." We think that the Park Service should reintroduce an updated version of the Light Brigade, with teams of college-educated media artists, naturalists and performers, to energize programs to reach park visitors.

We urgently need to protect Yosemite Valley and use it effectively to promote global conservation. Our National Parks keep the world on the right track.

–Richard Blair

The Lost Arrow at Sunset
Yosemite Valley

Upper Yosemite Falls at Dusk
Yosemite Valley

"National parks are the best idea we ever had. Absolutely American, absolutely democratic,
they reflect us at our best rather than our worst." –*Wallace Stegner*, 1983

FLOOD, HAPPY ISLES, 1969
Yosemite Valley

El Capitan Clearing a Storm, 1971
Yosemite Valley

YOSEMITE VALLEY AFTER
SPRING RAIN, 1991

Newborn Fawn

Chilnualna Falls
Wawona

Cathedral Rocks and the Merced River
Yosemite Valley

YOSEMITE VALLEY FROM THE DIVING BOARD

This photograph was retouched by the photographer to remove the
buildings, roads and bridges to show a more pristine view of Yosemite.

UPPER YOSEMITE FALLS
From Columbia Point

YOSEMITE FALLS FROM SUPERINTENDENT'S MEADOW, 1971
Yosemite Valley

The Minarets

THE NEVADA FALL

From John Muir, *The Yosemite*, 1912

The Nevada Fall is 600 feet high and is usually ranked next to the Yosemite in general interest among the five main falls of the Valley. Coming through the Little Yosemite in tranquil reaches, the river is first broken into rapids on a moraine boulder-bar that crosses the lower end of the Valley. Thence it pursues its way to the head of the fall in a rough, solid rock channel, dashing on side angles, heaving in heavy surging masses against elbow knobs, and swirling and swashing in pot-holes without a moment's rest. Thus, already chafed and dashed to foam, overfolded and twisted, it plunges over the brink of the precipice as if glad to escape into the open air. But before it reaches the bottom it is pulverized yet finer by impinging upon a sloping portion of the cliff about half-way down, thus making it the whitest of all the falls of the Valley, and altogether one of the most wonderful in the world.

On the north side, close to its head, a slab of granite projects over the brink, forming a fine point for a view, over its throng of streamers and wild plunging, into its intensely white bosom, and through the broad drifts of spray, to the river far below, gathering its spent waters and rushing on again down the cañon in glad exultation

Vernal and Nevada Falls
Glacier Point
Kathleen Goodwin

Top of Nevada Falls

into Emerald Pool, where at length it grows calm and gets rest for what still lies before it. All the features of the view correspond with the waters in grandeur and wildness. The glacier sculptured walls of the cañon on either hand, with the sublime mass of the Glacier Point Ridge in front, form a huge triangular pit-like basin, which, filled with the roaring of the falling river seems as if it might be the hopper of one of the mills of the gods in which the mountains were being ground.

Nevada Falls, Straight Down
Yosemite

EVERYTHING YOU NEED FOR COMFORT AND ENJOYMENT IN THE WILDERNESS CAN BE CARRIED IN A BACKPACK, ENABLING YOU TO CHOOSE YOUR OWN PATH AND MAKE YOUR OWN CAMPSITE. Entering the Sierra, you become part of an immense natural system and your senses become sharper. Your physical fitness and attitude will naturally improve, benefits you'll never get from watching other people's adventures on TV. Long hiking trips are tremendously stimulating. Besides, nothing is better than making love under the stars or in a hidden glade.

The Sierra is called "the gentle wilderness" because the weather is so perfect during the summer. The skies are achingly blue. It rarely rains at night, making camping much easier. Since the mountains are mostly granite, the soil is relatively root-resistant. The result is large areas of open grass and flower-covered meadows where one can hike off-trail. The water in the Sierra is clear and delicious, but you should always bring a purification filter for safety.

When backpacking, the lighter you go, the happier you'll be. Many experienced campers are able to get their packs down to fifteen pounds for a weekend hike! A few pages on, is a list of things you should consider taking on a summer Sierra backpacking trip. Everyone does it a little differently—one of our friends likes to backpack barefoot, but always brings a Sunday *New York Times* to read! Traveling as light as possible will enhance your experience, but don't omit the essentials: sun block, mosquito repellent, a flashlight, matches, and a basic first-aid kit with Band-Aids. A trip can be ruined by a bad sunburn or getting eaten alive by mosquitoes, nor will you have much fun if you can't make a fire or see in the dark. Hiking several miles a day can induce blisters—thus the Band-Aids for your toes and heels.

Of all the wild animals in the Sierra, bears are the most feared, but they're not interested in hurting you—they just want your food. To

DAVID VASSAR JUMPING FOR JOY
Cathedral Peak, Yosemite

protect yourself, your food, and the bears, you can buy or rent bear-proof containers. For the beginning backpacker, it's a good idea to go with more experienced friends or a group like the Sierra Club.

Too many hikers in one area can diminish the sense of being in the wilderness. Minimize your impact by having clothing and tent colors that blend in. As you gain confidence, you will find hidden places to experience true solitude and peace. If you are a good map reader and route finder, going off-trail is a way for you and your friends to really be alone. Solo travelers should always be extra careful to avoid an accident. Let someone know your route and return date.

Dogs (with dog backpacks) can be brought into national forests, but be sure to check the regulations first. Stores such as REI hold talks and classes to increase your outdoor skills. In time, some hikers become mountaineers (peak climbers) and rock climbers, while others learn kayaking and cross-country skiing. Winter hiking and ice climbing offer more delightful challenges to experienced mountaineers. Whatever your interests, please get out and enjoy the parks.

Years ago, I took a friend backpacking for the first time, hiking along a major river in the High Sierra. White granite peaks gleamed all around us. Eyeing a beautiful canyon off to our right, my friend asked where it led. "To the Sawtooth Range and Matterhorn Peak about twenty miles away," I replied, "but we're going down the river to see some waterfalls." My friend was incredulous. "You mean you can go anywhere you want?" It was as if a light suddenly flashed on inside his head—here was a place of magnificent beauty that seemingly went on forever. In that moment, he had grasped the endless possibilities of exploring the High Sierra.

We hope that by looking at our photographs you, too, will be inspired to experience the freedom and joy of being in the wilderness.

–Richard Blair

MT. GIBBS REFLECTED IN POND, WITH RAINDROPS
Yosemite
KATHLEEN GOODWIN

DOME TENT & RAINBOW
Tioga Pass

FATHER & SON
Half Dome From Glacier Point

THE TUOLUMNE RIVER DURING A SUMMER STORM

CLIMB THE MOUNTAINS AND GET THEIR GOOD TIDINGS. Nature's peace will flow into you as sunshine flows into trees. The winds will blow their own freshness into you and the storms their energy, while cares will drop off like autumn leaves.
    —*John Muir*, Our National Parks, 1901

BLACK BEAR SNIFFING FOR FOOD
Bridalveil Campground
Don't feed 'em!

CAMPFIRE AT DUSK

HANGING FOOD FROM A TREE
A safer method is to use a bear-proof container

NEWBORN FAWN
KATHLEEN GOODWIN

AUTHOR DOING A HEADSTAND ATOP MT. DANA
Yosemite High Sierra

CAMPGROUND BLUES

FAMILY WITH SMOKING FIRE

Camping in campgrounds is a gamble. You can find a quiet campsite among wildflowers by a creek, or be stuck next to a giant recreational vehicle with a generator running all night. Many campers don't know how to make a fire, so instead of making a small, cleanly burning blaze, their fires smolder all night, smelling like a belching bus. Loud motorcyclists blast though the campgrounds, while other inconsiderate campers play loud music from over-amped vehicles. The solution is walk-in campgrounds for nature lovers and landscaped parking lots for the RV crowd. Given that campgrounds can be so noisy and unhealthy, we have been forced to find an alternative.

GREEN CAMPING

Our method is what we call green camping, done when you want to sleep under the stars, simply and quietly. When twilight falls, park your car in a safe and private spot and take minimal camping equipment with you. Bring your insulated mat, sleeping bag, small pillow, mosquito repellent and flashlight in a medium-sized pack and hike a half-mile or so into the back country. Find a nice level spot and spread out the mat and sleeping bag. You'll have a wonderful night outdoors. Since you will be sleeping in a non-developed spot, you have major obligations. No fires to deface the site and get you noticed. No food to attract bears, raccoons, skunks, etc. If you sleep in the woods, it's your obligation to keep the site completely wild. No cutting branches or digging holes. Early in the morning, pack your few things into your pack and slip out to your car. Next, go to a picnic ground or restaurant for breakfast (and to use the facilities).

OFF-ROAD ETHICS

Many national forests contain an appalling mess of dirt tracks leading nowhere. Where four-wheel-drive and off-road vehicles are allowed, don't use the land as a hog wallow. Keep on the existing roads. TV commercials of actors happily plowing though the woods spraying dirt and crashing through streams are corporate crimes of the highest order. Real backcountry drivers, like those in Africa where Kathleen grew up, drive cautiously and slowly on outback roads, thus not ending up stuck in a dangerous situation and breaking an expensive machine. Mellow is better for you, the land and your property.

GO BACKPACKING!

Even if you're not an athlete, with a light pack and good gear you can put civilization behind you. Below is a list of stuff we bring. Everyone has different needs, but it's a start. Not everything on the list is essential, but you should think of the consequences of rain or snow at night. If you're in a high, exposed spot and there is a sudden storm, you must be prepared (the Boy Scout motto). We have seen swarms of mosquitoes that could drive a person mad and have had our pack taken by a mother bear and her cubs. Just take it one step at a time, balancing effort and enjoyment.

Sleeping bag	Moleskin or adhesive tape	Can opener or Swiss Army knife	Warm rainproof jacket
Pack	First-aid kit	Cleaning sponge	Camera
Therma-rest or sleeping pad	Little bit of wire	Thin nylon rope	Film or memory cards
Knife, fork, spoon	Food	Matches	Pillow
Toilet paper	Bear-proof container	Shorts	Wide-brim hat
Paper towels	Stove & fuel	Light pants	Compact binoculars
Toothbrush & toothpaste	Pots, cup & plate	T-shirts	Topo maps
Tent or tube tent	Sunglasses	Boots	Insect repellent
Flashlight	Batteries	Socks	Strong, good coffee & tea bags
Sunscreen	Ground cloth	Inner socks	Fun stuff

TUOLUMNE RIVER AND TUOLUMNE MEADOWS
Lembert Dome, Mt. Dana, and Kuna Crest are in the background.

INDIAN ACORN GRINDING HOLES, SENTINEL DOME, YOSEMITE VALLEY BELOW, 1970

JEFFREY PINE AND SENTINEL DOME, 1970
Yosemite High Sierra

MANY PEOPLE CANNOT AFFORD TO PAY THE ADMISSION FEES TO USE AND CAMP IN NATIONAL AND STATE PARKS. Think of teenagers and students whose first trips away from home are summer camping trips. Let's say a carload of kids, out of high school or college, decides to go off to see the national parks. If they stay in campgrounds at $15 a night and are out for a month, that's about $450 in camping fees. Add some entrance fees, and the price is looking more like apartment rent than pocket change. What about someone who has lost their job and needs to get away for a few days to regroup? Since parks heal people through exercise, fresh air and stress reduction, they are a necessity for the well-being of folks who are at risk from the wear and tear of urban living.

The idea of free parks, like Central Park in New York City, for example, is an old ideal, perhaps stemming from the exclusion of the commoners from the great estates of Europe.

The idea that land could be owned in common by the people of a community and every person could have access to it, at least in partnership with others, is a simple one and one that led to the establishment of the National Park Service and the system of state, county and regional parks. The benefits are obvious.

The imposition of fees to use these parks seems to be an accelerating trend in the past few years. It is a terrible idea to charge for park use, and one that should be abolished. The public has paid for these lands with their taxes. They belong to the public.

BUDD LAKE MOONRISE
Yosemite High Country

Everyone benefits from parks, not just the users. People who don't go to parks or can't backpack at least know that the parks are there. It's a mental escape from the strains of life.

The earth is at risk because of global warming, species extinction, pollution and the other horrors, right? Well, building an electorate that believes that the environment matters starts with park visits. If you're a nature lover, recycler, etc., how did you become one? I'll bet it was through visiting a park like Yosemite. If your parents couldn't afford to take you camping or even go on a picnic, imagine what that would have done to your beliefs.

Some people think that if park fees are high, it will preserve the parks by keeping out poor people. "They throw garbage around" some people think. What's a few extra dollars for rich people? Excluding people because they are ignorant of park etiquette is not the answer, education is! If rangers weren't running around hunting down fee-dodgers, they could spend their time teaching people how to enjoy parks responsibly. Park values have to be taught.

Who will pay for the parks? One ranger said to me, "If we had no backpacking fees, how would we pay for facilities?" The expense of the parks is a tiny part of the U.S., state or local budgets. There could be a voluntary collection of donations at park entrances. People who really love an area could endow a park.

At the very least, if a visitor says, "I can't afford this fee", the ranger should reply, "Welcome, our parks are for everyone, come on in!"

Chapter 4

The Eastside

The birds and animals, trees and grasses,
rocks, water and wind are our allies. They
waken our senses, rouse our passions,
renew our spirits and fill us with vision,
courage, and joy...

–David Gaines, Mono Lake activist

The Minarets and Lenticular Cloud

McGee Canyon

CALLED AMERICA'S DEEPEST VALLEY, THE EASTSIDE, AS WE CALL IT, OR THE OWENS VALLEY, STRETCHES FROM TOPAZ LAKE ON THE NEVADA BORDER IN THE NORTH TO BELOW LONE PINE IN ITS SOUTHERN EXTENT. The area is a long valley between the mighty Sierra and the almost equally high White Mountains to the east. The main road through the valley is Highway 395, which comes up from Los Angeles and down from Reno, connecting the various towns on the route.

The Sierra features a very steep side facing the Owens Valley, called an escarpment. These huge cliffs expose dazzling white rock, snow fields and glaciers. Side roads connect to steep trails, which rapidly take one to the high country wilderness via aspen-filled canyons with clear, cold, fast-moving streams. Indeed, the summit of Mt. Whitney, at 14,494 feet the highest point in the lower 48 states, can be reached from the Whitney Portal trailhead, which begins from a road that climbs to 9,000 feet. Many roads connect to trailheads, and a good map, plus a camping permit, will send you on your way.

Being in the rain shadow of the Sierra, the valley below is dry and desert-like. It has small towns to visit, including ghost towns, and an active Indian population, which has contributed everything from petroglyphs to casinos. A large ski community is based around Mammoth, with all the condos and lifts one would expect, but the hamlets, with their weathered buildings, swamp coolers, small schools, and local businesses, are also part of the rural quality the valley offers.

The area has good fishing, as many of the streams and lakes are stocked with trout.

ALABAMA HILLS AND THE SIERRA NEAR MT. WHITNEY
LONE PINE

Sailplanes and hang gliders ride the Sierra wave, a weather phenomenon where a smooth flow of air lifts over the mountain crest with strong, steady updrafts that glider pilots can ride for hours without engines. This wind also creates lenticular clouds.

Along the lower reaches of the rivers of the Eastside, cottonwood trees dip their roots into the water. These huge trees, as well as the aspens, turn a golden yellow that begs to be experienced in the fall. Winter brings snow to much of the valley, while the higher elevations get huge storms that close all roads, leaving the land ac- cessible only by cross-country ski or snowshoe. The White Mountains, much less well known and visited than the Sierra, are far dryer and hotter, but they have one of the most wonderful trees found on the planet, Bristlecone Pines, which are the oldest living things on earth.

Mono Lake is a huge, mysterious round lake just east of Yosemite National Park, a vast, shimmering inland sea of unusual alkaline water that supports a richness of life, particularly bird life. This lake was almost lost to Los Angeles' need for fresh water. It took decades of court fights to release the stranglehold the aqueduct had placed on the lake. LA's thirst for water transformed many of the rivers into dry beds of rock and sand and destroyed much of the farming in the area. Owens Lake, near the southern end of the valley where the Sierra subsides, is now a dry lake bed. Winds kick up clouds of dust full of minerals that irritate people's eyes and lungs, creating health problems that have driven many residents away. Los Angeles has recently been ordered to restore the lake, which should help the long-suffering ecology of the Eastside. To its credit, LA really is promoting and enforcing water conservation, and we can only hope that California's largest city will bring a more positive balance to the urban-rural equation.

The Eastside is one of California's great treasures. Visiting it is an outstanding way to reach the Sierra and White Mountains, as well as Death Valley, southeast of the Owens Valley.

THE SOUTHERN SIERRA AND OWENS LAKE
From Cerro Gordo Road
Owens Lake has been dry—a lake in name only—ever since Los Angeles began taking its water to fuel the growth of suburban development. Recent court rulings may restore enough water to solve problems caused by dust-borne mineral salts, which have damaged the health of local residents.

BRISTLECONE PINES IN THE WHITE MOUNTAINS

THE OLDEST LIVING ORGANISM KNOWN IS A BRISTLECONE PINE (*PINUS LONGAEVA*), NICKNAMED "METHUSELAH" AFTER THE LONGEST-LIVED CHARACTER IN THE BIBLE. Core samples have determined that this tree has been living in the White Mountains of eastern California for nearly 4,700 years. To protect the tree, the U.S. Forest Service does not reveal the exact location of "Methuselah" in the bristlecone grove. In 1964, a bristlecone even older than "Methuselah" was cut down by a graduate student doing research in an area now protected by Great Basin National Park in Nevada. The student had been taking core samples from the tree when his only coring tool broke, and the Forest Service allowed him to cut the ancient tree down. Posthumously named "Prometheus," the tree was found to be 4,862 years old by carefully counting each ring–no easy task, since the tree's trunk was very twisted and distorted. The death of "Prometheus" was not a total waste; the carbon content of the wood from its various rings was analyzed, providing an important calibration for radiocarbon dating.

Bristlecone pines grow in isolated groves at and just below tree-line. With cold temperatures, high winds, and short growing seasons, the trees grow very slowly. The wood is dense and resinous, and thus resistant to invasion by insects, fungi, and other potential pests. As the tree ages, much of its bark may die. In very old specimens, often only a narrow strip of living tissue is left to connect the roots to a handful of live branches.

THREE HORSES AND MT. TOM
Bishop

THE SERMON OF THE BLACK SHEEP
Lee Vining Canyon

COYOTE
Walker Creek

GREAT HORNED OWL
North of Bridgeport

MINER STOVE

CHILD'S BED FRAME WITH SOCKS

KITCHEN TABLE AND CHAIRS

WICKER CHAIR REMAINS
All pictures taken at Bodie State Historic Park

BODIE

Good-bye God, I'm going to Bodie!

Bodie Panorama

It is an easy leap from present-day California to the wild boom days of the 1870s in the ghost town of Bodie.

In 1859, Waterman Bodey and Blackie Taylor made one of the richest gold discoveries in the entire West. They called their find Taylor Gulch. At 8,300 feet in elevation, it was a desolate place that suffered terrible extremes of weather. Bodey himself fell victim to the first cruel winter, freezing to death while bringing supplies to the camp. Stricken with grief for his partner's death, Taylor sold his stake the following year. Their mining camp was named after Bodey but spelled Bodie to ensure correct pronunciation. A cave-in at Bodie's Bunker Hill Mine revealed a huge gold ore vein in 1877. The rush was on!

Over the next two years, Bodie grew from twenty inhabitants to 10,000. With more than 60 saloons and whorehouses, Bodie became notorious as the most lawless, wildest and toughest mining camp the Far West had ever known, where a killing was reputed to occur every day. The cry, *"Good-bye God, I'm going to Bodie"* was only half jest.

Mills churned around the clock, hastening the end of the boom. By 1882, only 500 men worked the mines, while the town's population dropped to several thousand. That summer, a tremendous fire swept through the main street of Bodie, destroying many houses that were never rebuilt. Another fire burned down the Standard Mine and Mill in 1898, but it was rebuilt the next year. The arrival of electrical power to run the machinery, and a new process using cyanide to extract small quantities of gold from the mill tailings, fanned hopes that the town might revive, but these improvements weren't enough. Bodie gradually faded away.

In 1932, a young boy named Bodie Bill started a fire while playing with matches in one of the old houses, sparking a conflagration that destroyed 90 percent of the remaining buildings. One last attempt to revive Bodie was made after World War II, but the newly built mill burned down before going into operation. As a working mining town, Bodie was finished.

In the end, more than $32 million in gold and $7 million in silver had been dug from Bodie's hills.

–Kathleen Goodwin

71

THE MYSTERIOUS SPIRES EMERGING FROM THE VAST WATERS OF MONO LAKE ARE CALLED "TUFA TOWERS."

Mono Lake is a sixty-five-square-mile lake in Owen's Valley, near the eastern border of Yosemite National Park. With no outlet, the water is very alkaline—nearly three times saltier than the ocean. Huge numbers of birds rely on Mono Lake, feeding on tiny brine shrimp and shore flies that thrive in the water and along the shoreline. Mono Lake is in Mono Basin, near Lee Vining, a small, funky desert town on Highway 395. This road links Los Angeles and Reno, and it is the main street of the Eastside.

The desert temperature around Mono Lake exceeds one hundred degrees in the summer, while in the winter, a dank, freezing fog often hangs in the basin for weeks on end. Most visitors come in summer, when the sky is wonderfully blue, to birdwatch, kayak, observe the islands Negit and Paoha in the middle of the lake, and marvel at the strange formations of limestone sticking out of the water. These tufa towers, made of calcium carbonate, are formed when the alkaline lake water interacts with the fresh spring water in the tributaries that feed Mono Lake. The lake is one of the oldest in the United States, known to have been in existence at least 760,000 years.

Mark Twain (Samuel Clemens) wrote about a boat excursion to the islands of Mono Lake in "Roughing It," the story of his adventures in the West. His boat almost sank during a terrific storm that came up:

"We were evidently in serious peril, for the storm had greatly augmented; the billows ran very high and were capped with foaming crests, the heavens were hung with black, and the wind blew with great fury. We would have gone back, now, but we did not dare to turn the boat around, because as soon as she got in the trough of the sea she would upset, of course. Our only hope lay in keeping her head on to the seas. It was hard work to do this, she plunged so, and so beat and belabored the billows with her rising and falling bows. Now and then one of Higbie's oars would trip on the top of a wave, and the other one would snatch the boat half around in spite of my cumbersome steering apparatus. We were drenched by the sprays constantly, and the boat occasionally shipped water.

Just as the darkness shut down we came booming into port, head on. Higbie dropped his oars to hurrah—I dropped mine to help—the sea gave the boat a twist, and over she went!

The agony that alkali water inflicts on bruises, chafes and blistered hands, is unspeakable, and nothing but greasing all over will modify it—but we ate, drank and slept well, that night, notwithstanding."

In the West, water has always meant wealth—first for agriculture and later for land developers. Water made it possible to turn the parched, empty deserts into sprawling suburbs and high-priced luxury homes. As Los Angeles sought to expand in the years before World War II, its Department of Water and Power quietly bought up water rights to most of the Owens Valley, then began pumping the water south via aqueduct in 1941. (The story of ranchers versus developers was dramatized in the acclaimed movie *Chinatown*, starring Jack Nicholson.)

Four of the five rivers that fed Mono Lake were diverted to the aqueduct, with predictable results: by the 1970s, the lake was dying of dehydration. Ornithologist and bird lover David Gains became concerned. Ninety percent of the state's California Gull population breeds each winter on islands protected by Mono Lake, and if the water level kept falling, coyotes would soon be able reach these former islands to eat the eggs in the nests. Alarmed that the entire population of gulls was at risk, Gains formed a committee dedicated to halting the excessive diversion of water from Mono Lake. In 1983, the Mono Lake Committee won a major victory when the California Supreme Court ruled that

the state was obliged to protect places like Mono Lake even if past water allocation decisions had to be reconsidered. The following year, the Mono Lake Committee joined the National Audubon Society and California Trout in suing Los Angles, claiming that these water diversions did not comply with the California Fish and Game codes. Ten years later, the California Water Resources Board set limits on the amount of water that could be exported from Mono Lake, stabilizing the water level and protecting the nesting gulls. Los Angeles was also ordered to restore the streams and waterfowl habitat. The Mono Lake Committee successfully lobbied for funds to help Los Angeles develop recycling facilities and pay for water conservation programs. Los Angeles is now one the nation's leaders in water conservation.

Tufa Tower Reflections
Mono Lake State Reserve

MONO LAKE IN WINTER
Northern Shore

SUN CUPS IN SNOW, MONO LAKE FROM 13,053 FEET
Summit, Mt. Dana
KATHLEEN GOODWIN

75

FALES HOT SPRINGS, WINTER
North of Bridgeport
(Not open to the public, undeveloped, hot water in its natural state)

KEOGH HOT SPRINGS
Nine miles south of Bishop

HIDDEN HOT SPRINGS

THE EASTSIDE IS A HOTBED OF GEOTHERMAL ACTIVITY BECAUSE OF POOLS OF MOLTEN ROCK BELOW THE GROUND. As water from rivers, rain, or snow makes its way underground, it is heated by the hot rocks below and turned to steam or hot water. The heating causes an increase in pressure, forcing the water back to the surface as a hot spring or a geyser.

Hot springs are common in the Eastside and some, like Keogh, are plumbed into a swimming pool; others are constructed by a core group of (hippie) nature lovers. They dig out soaking pools, come up with schemes to regulate the temperature, and decorate the pools with local stones or pottery inset into hand-trowelled retaining walls. Most commercial mineral baths require a swimsuit, while hippie hot springs are clothing-optional.

What you wear or don't wear is up to you, but if there are drunks or toughs in the area, use common sense.

Always check the water carefully before going in—hot springs vary wildly in temperature and people have been badly burned in violent steam and boiling water cauldrons. But don't be scared off—hot springs are wonderfully rejuvenating and almost everyone is totally mellow.

Memorial at Manzanar

Folded Crane Origami
Manzanar

MANZANAR–A JAPANESE RELOCATION CAMP

Manzanar War Relocation Center was one of ten camps in which Japanese American citizens and resident Japanese aliens were imprisoned during World War II. Located at the foot of the Sierra Nevada in eastern California's Owens Valley, Manzanar is the best preserved of these camps. Visitors can wander at will or take a three-mile drive around the camp using a descriptive map available at the site's interpretive center.

It is difficult today to understand the intensity of the anti-Japanese feelings generated by the Japanese bombing of Pearl Harbor during World War II and Japanese wartime atrocities. Most of the Japanese people living in the United States were arrested and put in these prison camps for the duration of the war. Many lost their homes, land, and businesses, even though they'd done nothing to support the Japanese government's war on the United States. In effect, they were punished for their ethnic background. Published stories and artwork remain of the time the Japanese spent in Manzanar, and relics of the camps are all over the site. It is a sad place, still visited by many relatives of those interned in camps and others who have an interest in history and civil rights.

Remains of Japanese Garden Steps
Manzanar

MT. WHITNEY AT SUNRISE

Chapter 5

Death Valley

Death Valley is, ironically, about the persistence of life.

In Twenty-Mule-Team Canyon

DEATH VALLEY SURELY CONFIRMS OUR THESIS THAT CALIFORNIA IS A LAND OF EXTREMES. Not only does it have the highest mountain in the lower 48 states, the tallest and oldest trees, but also the hottest place on earth—Death Valley in the summer. Temperatures on the ground can reach 180 degrees Fahrenheit. Death Valley attracts thrill-seeking tourists who come to experience this extreme heat. They rely on their car's air-conditioning systems and try not to spend too much time unprotected in the noonday sun. More intelligent explorers of the desert, who sometimes refer to themselves as desert rats,

know better, and visit Death Valley and other arid regions in California when cooler temperatures prevail. While northern California is lashed by winter rains, southern California deserts can be in the 80s and 90s, perfect places to enjoy warmth in the winter while taking in the awesome scenery comfortably. The desert offers solitude, clarity of vision from the low humidity of the air, enormous night skies. With its graphic, uncluttered beauty and few people, Death Valley is the perfect antidote to modern living.

As soon as one enters the park one must keep in mind the basics of survival, so it seems

fitting that in 1933 the original construction of the park, its camps, roads, and buildings, was built by the Civilian Conservation Corps. This program provided a basic living for hundreds of unemployed young men during the Depression. More than 1,200 civilians worked in the park until 1942, when many were called up for service in World War II.

Death Valley National Park covers more than 3.3 million acres of land. The lowest point in the western hemisphere is at Badwater, 282 feet below sea level. Nearly 550 square miles of the park are below sea level. The valley is bounded on the

THE SALT PAN OF DEATH VALLEY AND TELESCOPE PEAK
Seen from Dante's View

west by Telescope Peak (11,049 feet and frequently snow-covered) and on the east by Dante's View (5,475 feet) (see above). The valley floor is about 200 miles long and has numerous side canyons to explore. Some require four-wheel drive, like the exceptional 28-mile one-way drive through Titus Canyon, but many are accessible in a regular car if the weather is good and care is taken. Titus Canyon has startling views of huge canyons.

The main campground in Death Valley is pretty stark, just rows of RVs with no vegetation to hide them or stop the blowing sand. However, it is legal to camp anywhere in the park if you are two miles from the paved road. So, with a spirit of adventure, it is possible to find a side road and a peaceful and unique view of this surreal landscape.

We have evolved our own way of experiencing these immense vistas. We drive up to Dante's View, for example, and then one of us will coast down on a bicycle while the other drives our car behind to protect the cyclist. We have a prearranged signal (we hoot the horn) so that if another car comes along and wants to pass, we both pull over. One time I rode a bicycle from the top of the Panamint range all the way down to Death Valley. A curious pair of ravens flew above me for miles. I could see their shadows preceding me on the road. Sometimes they would fly ahead, gliding on the warm air. I felt like I was flying with them as I "flew" down the road and they soared overhead, calling to each other.

Artist's Palette

83

Park Bench on Zabriskie Point, Sunset

We have taken turns riding down extraordinary roads all over the West. We don't get fit, but the visuals are amazing.

Death Valley boasts the second-highest air temperature ever recorded—134 degrees Fahrenheit in 1913. It was given its name by gold-seekers, some of whom died crossing the valley during the 1849 California Gold Rush. As in all deserts, if the people had known where to find water they would not have died. Such a place is Saratoga Springs in the southeast corner of the valley. One walks up to a saddle between two hills, looks over the ridge, and sees three adjoining pools of water encircled with golden reeds and birds feeding at their shores. I can only imagine the exquisite relief such a sight of six acres of clear, fresh water must have been to travelers in the past.

Rock drawings, campsites and foot trails from prehistoric hunters and gatherers are found in almost every part of the valley.

More than 1,000 kinds of plants live within the park. Some have roots that reach down 50 feet, or their root systems lie just below the surface but extend out in all directions. Others have leaves and stems that allow very little evaporation of water.

The desert can come alive with flowers in the spring, particularly if there has been a good winter rain, which is quite rare. Rangers in Death Valley can advise when to visit for the best colors.

–Kathleen Goodwin

Bloom, Death Valley

84

HIKER IN THE HEAT
Golden Canyon

EUREKA DUNES

BADWATER, LOWEST SPOT IN THE WESTERN HEMISPHERE

UBEHEBE CRATER

PETE AGUEREBERRY'S BUICK, SHOT UP

PETE AGUEREBERRY, GOLD MINER AND DESERT LOVER

PETE AGUEREBERRY DID NOT HAVE AN AUS-PICIOUS START IN DEATH VALLEY. He nearly died trying to cross the valley. He was discovered and nursed back to health. In 1905 he and prospector Shorty Harris discovered gold and named the spot Harrisberry. Shorty later took full credit for the strike and renamed the town Harrisburg. There are no remains of Harrisburg, which at one time supported 300 people. Two miles east of it, Pete worked his claim at the Eureka Mine until his death in 1945. The remains of the elaborate systems he made to remove gold can still be seen. While exploring the ruins, we spotted Pete's Buick in the valley below.

Nearby the mine, Pete's house and out-buildings are also still standing and reveal a man of taste who wanted to make his life comfortable and aesthetic. There is flowered wallpaper in his home and the view from the fire pit out front is stunning. It is easy to conjure up the scene of the miners enjoying an evening under the stars after working all day in the depths of the earth.

Pete built by hand the road to what is known now as Aguereberry's Point (6,433 feet) so that his visitors could also share the spectacular view of Mount Charleston (11,900 feet) eighty miles to the east in Nevada and the valley below, with its green oasis of Furnace Creek and white salt flats of Badwater Basin.

SUNRISE AT AGUEREBERRY POINT

Sandstorm, Twenty-Mule-Team Canyon

91

Ibex Pass and Sand Dunes

CHARCOAL KILNS
Wildrose

SARATOGA SPRINGS
Salt Creek Area, Southern Death Valley

WILD BURROS

KEENE WONDER MINE

Chapter 6

The Salton Sea,
Joshua Tree and
Mohave National Parks

Life not crowded upon life as in other places but scattered abroad in spareness and simplicity.

–Edward Abbey

Joshua Trees and Desert Bloom
Kathleen Goodwin

White Pelicans (bump on beaks appear on males in breeding season)

Salton Sea Sunset with Pelican

The Salton Sea is the largest lake in California. It was created when the All-American Canal, a project to divert the Colorado River from Mexico, broke its banks; the flooding could not be stopped for two years! It has a huge fish and bird population, and birds depend on it during their annual migration. Its waters are contaminated with fertilizer and pesticide runoff from Imperial Valley irrigation. Periodically, vast algae blooms rapidly use up the oxygen in the lake, and millions of fish die, as seen here. The Salton Sea even had an era as a seaside resort. People who like dry heat still live there.

This Salt Is My Salt

THE BEACHES ARE COVERED WITH DEAD FISH AFTER AN ALGAE BLOOM.

Mohave

Kelso
Mohave

JOSHUA TREE & MOJAVE NATIONAL PARKS

Joshua trees, with their spiky leaves and furry bark, are so unusual that unscrupulous realtors stuck oranges on the spikes in an attempt to sell land to dazed newcomers arriving on the new transcontinental railroad!

Joshua Tree National Park is located in southeastern California. Declared a U.S. National Park in 1994, it was previously a national monument. The park includes 1,200 square miles of land. Seventy-five percent of the park is wilderness area. The park includes parts of two deserts, each an ecosystem whose characteristics are determined primarily by elevation. Below 3,000 feet, the Colorado Desert encompasses the eastern part of the park and features natural gardens of creosote bush, ocotillo, and cholla cactus. The Little San Bernardino Mountains run through the southwest edge of the park.

The higher, moister, and slightly cooler Mojave Desert is the special habitat of the Joshua tree, from which the park gets its name. In addition to Joshua tree forests, the western part of the park includes some of the most interesting geologic displays found in California's deserts. The dominant geologic features of this landscape are hills of bare rock, usually broken up into loose boulders. These hills are enjoyable for rock climbing and scrambling. The flatland between these hills is sparsely forested with Joshua trees. Together with the boulder piles, the trees make the landscape otherworldly. Five fan palm oases in the park are the few areas where water occurs naturally and wildlife abounds.

At least 240 species of birds have been observed in the park. A good place to view wildlife is at Barker Dam, a short hike from a parking area near Hidden Valley. Desert Bighorn Sheep sometimes stop by the dam for a drink.

FOUNTAIN PEAK
Providence Mountains, Mohave Desert

JOSHUA TREE AND SUN

Newspaper Clippings in Abandoned Mining Cabin
near Mojave National Preserve

FLOWERING YUCCA
Joshua Tree N.P.

BACK LIT CHOLLA
Mojave Desert

BEAVER TAIL CACTUS IN BLOOM

THE FLOWER OF THE JOSHUA TREE
Mojave Desert

Joshua Tree National Park

Chapter 7

San Francisco

One day if I do go to heaven...I'll look around and
say, 'It ain't bad, but it ain't San Francisco'.

–Herb Caen

GOLDEN GATE BRIDGE AND TRANSAMERICA PYRAMID, SUNSET
from Marin Headlands, Golden Gate National Recreation Area

SPEED: AN AMERICA'S CUP SAILBOAT
WITH AN EVEN FASTER WINDSURFER

Tugboat, Ferry and Sailboat in the Fog
San Francisco City Front from Oakland

110

Fishing Boats *Tamile, Romance, Phu Quy,*
with Telegraph Hill and Coit Tower

Dungeness Crab

FISHERMAN'S WHARF

San Francisco is a real city. It's not touting its faded charms. The beauty of its locale beside the bay, the Victorian architecture, cable cars and the legendary tolerance of its residents combine to produce the most beautiful city in the country. It draws more tourists than any other American city but still manages to be a real place where people enjoy living. It's multi-ethnic and multi-sexual!

The wharf started as an open air fisherman's market where San Franciscans in the know bought fresh fish right off the fishing boats. Now it's the area most overrun with souvenir shops. However, the classic fisherman's wharf meal, Dungeness crab and sourdough bread, ain't so bad. Neither is an Irish Coffee (with hot coffee, a little sugar, and Irish whiskey, topped with extra-heavy cream) served at the Buena Vista Bar, near the end of the cable car tracks. It keeps the fog away.

Look out across the bay. Some mystical force of nature pulls us to observe the waters, the lights, the fog. We watch the boats, and the seals, in turn, watch us. Get out on the water. From the marinas or the Ferry Building, ships await to take you sailing around the bay, or on a ferry ride to Alcatraz, Sausalito, Oakland or Vallejo.

GRIPMAN WITH THE TOOLS OF THE TRADE
*The gripman uses the lever to clamp to
a cable running under the street which
provides propulsion for the cable car.*

NIGHT RUN

DETAIL OF BELL-RINGING CORD AND COLORED
GLASS CLERESTORY

A CABLE CAR IS STILL A FORM   OF TRANSPORTATION...

CABLE CARS
Go halfway to the stars...

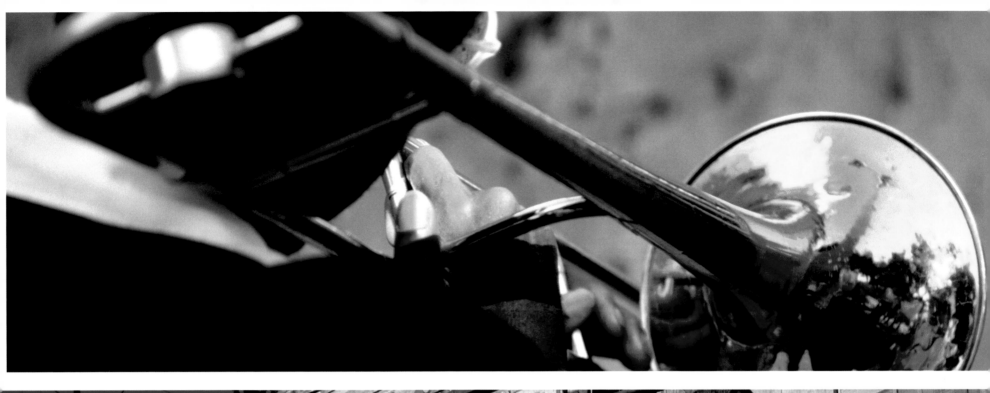

From upper left:

Slide Trombonist at Beach Street

Rollerbladers and Joggers, JFK Drive on Sunday

Stilt walker, SF Carnival

Vivian and Marian Brown, The Famous Identical Twins of SF

Murals at Balmy Alley

Carnaval Dancers
The Mission
Kathleen Goodwin
(Both Pages)

C
A
R
N
A
V
A
L
S.
F.

Carnaval San Francisco is the largest multicultural festival in California

Cocktail Waitresses

The Twins

Act-Up AIDS Activists

Rhinestone Jewelry
Kathleen Goodwin

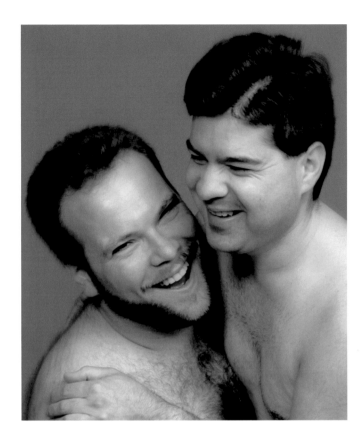 

SAN FRANCISCO IS THE GAY CAPITAL OF THE WORLD. It is the world's most popular destination for gay tourists and each June hosts San Francisco Pride, the world's best-known gay pride parade and festival. The city tried to legalize gay marriage, and weddings were performed here until the California Supreme Court forbade it. The largest concentration of gay men and lesbians in the world lives in the San Francisco Bay Area. The freedom that they have is a wonderful thing. Here we have gay bars, nightclubs, bookstores, and lots of other businesses geared for gays, plus many of San Francisco's businesses of all kinds are run and owned by gays. We are getting a *lot* of the world's talent.

We also wish to include people with other sexual preferences: bisexuals, transgender, metrosexuals, everyone! (If we left out your kink, please stay calm.)

It is a crime when consenting adults are not allowed to express their sexuality. People who are not hetrosexual are punished for it—in some countries with death. Those who are freaked out by the scene certainly don't need to deal with it. However, the feeling we get from the city's gayness is one of relaxed fun. Of course the downside of unprotected sex is AIDS and other STD's but *most* of San Francisco is in the forefront of safe sex and public health care. *Please be careful*, as everyone, straight, gay and in-between, is at risk!

ROWBOAT, STOW LAKE
Golden Gate Park, San Francisco

GOLDEN GATE PARK

The spiritual home of many San Franciscans, Golden Gate Park is both a natural refuge and a cultural resource. Like many of its visitors, the park has undergone a major metamorphosis. Originally covered with sand dunes, it was designed by a civil engineer, William Hammond Hall. He appointed landscape gardener John McClaren as director, a position McClaren held for fifty years. McClaren transformed the park by emptying the manure sweepings of the city streets onto the thousand acres of sand dunes until the humus lay at least a foot thick. The park now has eleven lakes, more than a million trees, museums, riding stables, a carousel and miles of hiking and biking trails.

DANCING GIRL AND SANDCASTLE
Maritime Museum

CONSERVATORY OF FLOWERS

SPEEDWAY MEADOWS
Golden Gate Park, San Francisco

At one time, North Beach was an actual beach, but it was later filled in to create the land that it is today.

Italian settlers were the first to populate the area, which remains a largely Italian neighborhood, with many wonderful Italian restaurants, cafes, and gelato parlors. Joe Dimaggio, "The Yankee Clipper," grew up and learned to play baseball in North Beach, then returned later with his wife, Marilyn Monroe.

Beat poets Allen Ginsberg, Neal Cassady, Lawrence Ferlinghetti, Gary Snyder, Philip Whalen, Jack Kerouac, Michael McClure, and Kenneth Rexroth found a home in North Beach, where they helped established the legendary City Lights bookstore. Just off Columbus Avenue, you can find an alleyway named for Jack Kerouac.

In recent years, Chinatown has expanded into North Beach, adding to the incredible variety of local restaurants.

TROLLEY CAR WIRES WITH ST. PETER AND PAUL CHURCH
North Beach

CITY LIGHTS BOOKSTORE
Corner of Columbus and Broadway

SIGN FOR VESUVIO'S,
San Francisco saloon enjoyed by the Beat poets.

COIT TOWER

CHEERY FLOWER SELLERS
San Francisco

HERBAL SHOP
Grant Avenue, San Francisco

CHILD IN LAUNDRY WITH GRANDMOTHER

RIDING THE CABLE CAR
San Francisco

Chinatown begins in downtown San Francisco at the Dragon Gate on the corner of Bush Street and Grant Avenue with a plethora of restaurants and shops. Stockton Street, one block west, has a more authentic Chinese character, reminiscent of Hong Kong, with its produce and fish markets, stores and restaurants. Chinatown has smaller side streets and interesting alleyways. Portsmouth Square is one of the few open spaces in Chinatown; it bustles with people doing Tai Chi and Chi Gung and old men playing Chinese chess.

The first Chinese immigrants came as laborers to build California's railroads or as miners hoping to strike it rich during the Gold Rush. As many settled in San Francisco, racial tensions boiled over into full-blown race riots, prompting the Chinese residents to form the Consolidated Chinese Benevolent Association to collectively strengthen their political power and economic power, Through the association, new immigrants could locate people from their native districts, socialize, receive monetary aid, and express opinions in community affairs.

The Chinese Exclusion Act of 1882 further restricted Chinese immigration to single males, encoding racism into law. This was the first immigration law ever aimed at a single ethnic group in America; it lingered on the books until its repeal during the Second World War.

Chinatown was completely destroyed in the 1906 earthquake and fire that leveled the city. Much of the rebuilt area seen today was planned and developed with an eye toward tourism. While Chinatown continues to receive new immigrants who help maintain its lively and active character, the neighborhood remains relatively poor and its population increasingly elderly as upwardly mobile younger Chinese leave for suburbia and more affluent areas. Many have settled in the outlying Richmond and Sunset districts of San Francisco, creating new Asian neighborhoods.

THE STREET OF GAMBLERS (ROSS ALLEY)
Arnold Genthe, 1898

CHINESE GENTLEMAN
Grant Avenue

NEW YEAR'S FIREWORKS

125

Transamerica Pyramid with Moon

TRANSAMERICA PYRAMID AND COLUMBUS AVENUE

Photographed from a small plane that rolled 100 degrees so Richard could get a straight down view. He said afterward it was the 'falling down view.'

PYRAMID FACTS AND FIGURES

Number of floors: 48

Largest Floor: The fifth, measuring 145 feet per side and containing 21,025 square feet of space

Smallest floor: the 48th, measuring only 45 feet per side and containing 2,025 square feet of space

Total space: 530,000 square feet

Total height: 853 feet, including the 212-foot spire

Number of elevators: 18, with two reaching the top floor

Number of windows: 3,678

Type of base: Four-level, multi-use, including lobby, restaurant and garage

Base: Approximately 16,000 cubic yards of concrete, encasing more than 300 miles of steel reinforcing rods.

Exterior material: White precast quartz aggregate

Excavation began: December 1969

Depth of excavation: 52 feet

First steel placed: November 1970

First occupancy: Summer 1972

Number of people working in the Pyramid: More than 1,500, employed by more than 50 firms

Architect: William L. Pereira

FULL MOON AT THE GIANTS' NEW STADIUM
San Francisco
KATHLEEN GOODWIN

Barry Bonds

Barry Lamar Bonds (born July 24, 1964 in Riverside, California) came to play left field for the San Francisco Giants in 1993. A prodigious hitter, Bonds holds the single-season record for most home runs with 73, and as of this writing remains second only to Hank Aaron in career homers. The only player in baseball history to hit 500 home runs and steal 500 bases, Bonds won the National League's Most Valuable Player Award a record seven times and is considered among the greatest players in baseball history. Many of the game's best players, hitters and pitchers alike, remain in awe of Bonds's bat speed and dominance at the plate. He is one of only four players in major league history to be intentionally walked with the bases loaded.

As of this writing, his record is under a cloud, due to alleged problems with performance-enhancing drugs.

BARRY BONDS

One of the wildest characters in baseball was the fiercely competitive Billy Martin. Legendary as a player for his readiness to fight on and off the field, Billy lost none of that fire later in life when he returned to his boyhood home to manage the Oakland A's. He knew the rules of baseball inside and out, and made sure *the opposing team* adhered to the letter of the law by shouting at the umpires whenever he spotted an infraction. His aggressive approach to the game emphasized speed and quickness on the base paths, a style that became known as *Billy Ball* and led the A's to win their division in 1981.

During a game against the California Angels in late April of that year, one of the Angels batters was accused of using an illegal "corked" bat. When the batter resisted showing it to the umpire, Billy ran out on the field to grab the bat. Both dugouts emptied and a huge fight broke out. I took these pictures with a telephoto lens from the roof of the visiting team's dugout.

FIGHTING TO INSPECT THE BAT
Oakland Coliseum

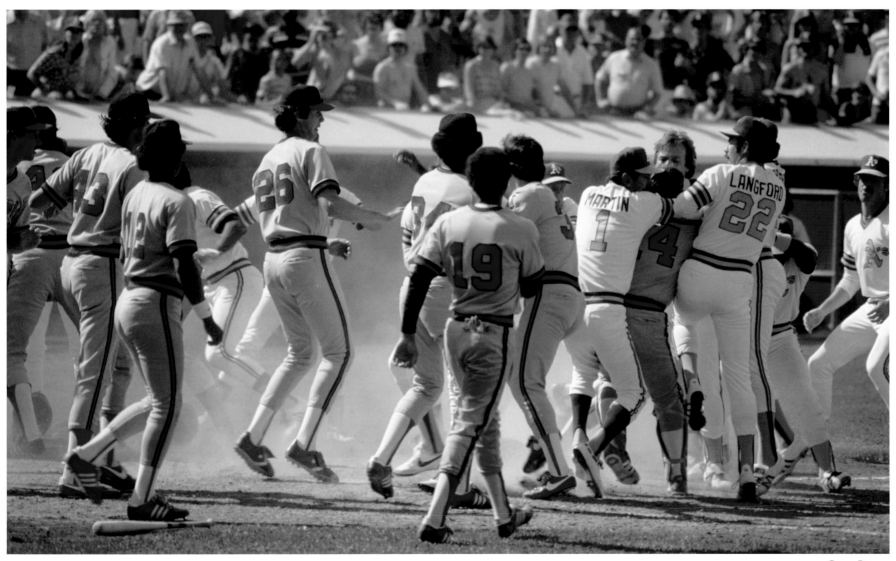

BILLY BRAWL
Oakland Coliseum

Chapter 8

Los Angeles & Hollywood

Hollywood is a place where they'll pay you a thousand dollars for a kiss and fifty cents for your soul.

– Marilyn Monroe

THEME BUILDING
Los Angeles Airport

THE HEART OF THE CITY IS ITS PEOPLE, AND LOS ANGELENOS ARE A BREED APART. As a group, they exude a wonderful energy, with casual yet stylish dress, and they talk with a sly underlying sarcasm easy to mistake for shallowness. Later, you realize they were just making fun of themselves and the inherent absurdity of living in the pulsing heart of the Dream Factory.

Led by the film and television industry, Los Angeles has managed to find a way to thrive through good times and bad. Much of this success is fueled by the relentless influx of young people from all over America and the world, eager to employ their skills and energy in this constantly evolving economy. Some are highly educated computer experts, others illegal aliens, but they all come for the same basic reason: to make a better

life for themselves and their families. In a nation of immigrants, Los Angeles may be the most diverse major city of all. As with any elemental force, immigration is a double-edged sword. It supplies the energy, fresh ideas, and willingness to work essential to a growing economy. At the same time, this tide of people has inevitably strained our already over-

stressed medical systems, intensifying problems of unemployment, substandard wages, and a lack of affordable housing–problems we have not yet begun to address, let alone solve. It's a safe bet, however, that the very people whose presence has exacerbated these problems will in the end be an integral part of the solutions. Without the willingness of immigrants, legal or otherwise, to do the hard work essential to maintaining our economic foundations, the good life so many Californians enjoy would quickly turn to dust.

For us, the best thing about Los Angeles is the city's vast, multicultural population and the

CHILIES FOR SALE

wonderful experiences this diversity provides both visitor and resident alike. Who wouldn't enjoy the choice of dining out at Japanese, Jewish, Thai, Vietnamese, Indian,

Korean, Chinese, Soul Food, Italian, Mexican, South and Central American, Russian, or French restaurants? Add the wide variety of festivals, ethnic goods, and musical performances available to anyone with a sense of adventure, and the city becomes a world destination. The issue of ethnicity can be one of pleasure and learning rather than distrust and fear.

It's all here in Los Angeles, from the prefabricated fast food chains that litter the urban landscape to exclusive and very expensive restaurants run by celebrity chefs, where the most powerful film industry executives and movie stars come to be seen and pampered. Between these extremes lie the hidden treasures, family-run restaurants that express the unique essence of Los Angeles in the form of food–places like Pink's, famous for its chili-smothered hot dogs since 1939, or the Musso and Frank Grill, serving steaks, chops, and legendary martinis to a clientele ranging from ordinary citizens to Hollywood insiders, for almost ninety years.

GETTY CAFE
Kathleen Goodwin

Watts Towers
designed and built by
Simon Rodia
*Idiosyncratic, exuberant,
monumental urban art.*

135

VINCENT PRICE BACKSTAGE AFTER PERFORMING *The Raven* BY EDGAR ALLAN POE.

KODAK CF 1000 5(

HOLLYWOOD

On Location in Chinatown

Disney Studio Street Sign

Raising the Flag (a reflector) in LA

137

IT'S EASY TO DISMISS MOVIE STARS AS MERE POP ICONS, BUT OUR CURRENT GOVERNOR IS ARNOLD SCHWARZENEGGER, STAR OF THE TERMINATOR MOVIES. Our most famous actor-turned-politician was Ronald Reagan, who left Hollywood to become Governor of California, then was elected to two terms as President of the United States. In the age of television, the commercial entertainment industry is a sophisticated and ruthlessly professional mind-control industry selling over-consumption, fear, and simplistic, feel-good politics. To that end, Hollywood brought us the test screening, the focus group, the sound bite, the spin—and now it brings us our presidents, our wars, even our self-images. It's all up there on the screen: what we do, where we go, what we buy, how we make love, and when frustrations boil over, how we shoot our neighbors. Hollywood has always glorified the heroics of guns and war with the fantasy super-hero, played by Schwarzenegger, Stallone or Mel Gibson. These stars are invulnerable and they kill our current enemy (normally Asian, now Arab) with ease and humor. Many notable Hollywood personalities are Democrats and have been vocal in their political beliefs, but the big money from the Republican right wing pushes its candidates for elected office.

The stars we see on screen represent only the tip of a vast entertainment industry. Behind every smiling actor stands an unseen army of highly skilled technicians, from make-up artists and wardrobe people to the lighting, grip, and camera crews who do the heavy lifting essential for every film production. These hard-working people truly are "the man behind the curtain." Without them, there would be no Hollywood.

Los Angeles is the second-largest major manufacturing center in the United States, but filmmaking remains its signature industry.

The influence of the movies on world culture is incalculable, drawing talented people from across the globe to the melting pot of Hollywood, where they add their skills to the growing fusion of creativity and technology that is the modern film industry.

REPUBLICAN-THEMED MOVIE THEATRE

ANTHONY QUINN MURAL, DOWNTOWN, BY ELOY TORREZ, ASSISTED BY BOB GRIGAS

138

FLOODED VALLEY

Harrison Ford narrating a film proposing the restoration of Hetch Hetchy to its natural state. Before it was flooded, this valley rivalled Yosemite Valley in beauty and majesty. If the land was restored, water and power users could get their needs met downstream, and the National Park Service would regain one of its finest landscapes.

HETCH HETCHY DAM

FORD AND DIRECTOR DAVID VASSAR

It's great when a popular film actor is on the side of the environment.

HARRISON FORD
Hetch Hetchy Dam in Yosemite

It's easy to be overwhelmed by Los Angeles highways. Back in the 60s, freeways offered the freedom of the open road, taking you anywhere in less than half an hour. Now, the freeways are anything but free, and have become emblematic of all that's wrong with LA. The endless streams of cars drive faster and closer together than in the rest of the state, adding a dangerous edge. That sense of danger is no illusion: high-speed congestion inevitably leads to accidents as drivers jockey for any open patch of road. Fender-benders are common during rush hours.

Any problem lacking workable solutions will inevitably get worse, so it was no surprise when the rising tide of frustration led to the first outbreaks of spontaneous freeway shootings on LA freeways during the mid-1980s, car-to-car gunfire that periodically erupts to this day. When tempers flare, the results—road rage and bloody accidents—can be tragic.

According to urban legend, more than forty percent of LA's land mass is devoted to cars. This includes roads, parking lots, freeways, and "cloverleaf" intersections, where thousands of tons of concrete and steel arc through the air to join one freeway to another. Are they earthquake safe? Not all of them.

The roads themselves can threaten the safety of an unwary driver. The Pasadena Freeway was built in 1940, designed to handle a light traffic load of vehicles traveling a maximum speed of 45 mph. This antiquated roadway is in heavy use today. Exiting the freeway means that a car traveling well above the posted 55 mph must negotiate a hairpin bend at 5 miles an hour. Fortunately, the people of LA pirouette very gracefully.

With miles of congested driving required to get anywhere, going from one end of LA to the other must be a well-timed excursion. Events take on importance due to the time and effort required to get there.

Driving a car can be a real pleasure in California, but it's a guilty pleasure at best here in LA—and no pleasure at all during rush hour, when the crush of cars exceeds a critical mass. The term "smog" was coined in Los Angeles, but newer cars with improved fuel emissions and more stringent pollution controls on factories, have made a real difference in atmospheric contamination. The skies of LA remain dangerously polluted, but long-time residents will tell you that their air is much cleaner now than it was thirty years ago.

Electric cars for urban use and car-free shopping streets might help. But we are artists, not urban planners or dictators, so Los Angeles will have to sort itself out. Enjoy the photographs and come up with your own plan for urban transit or levitation.

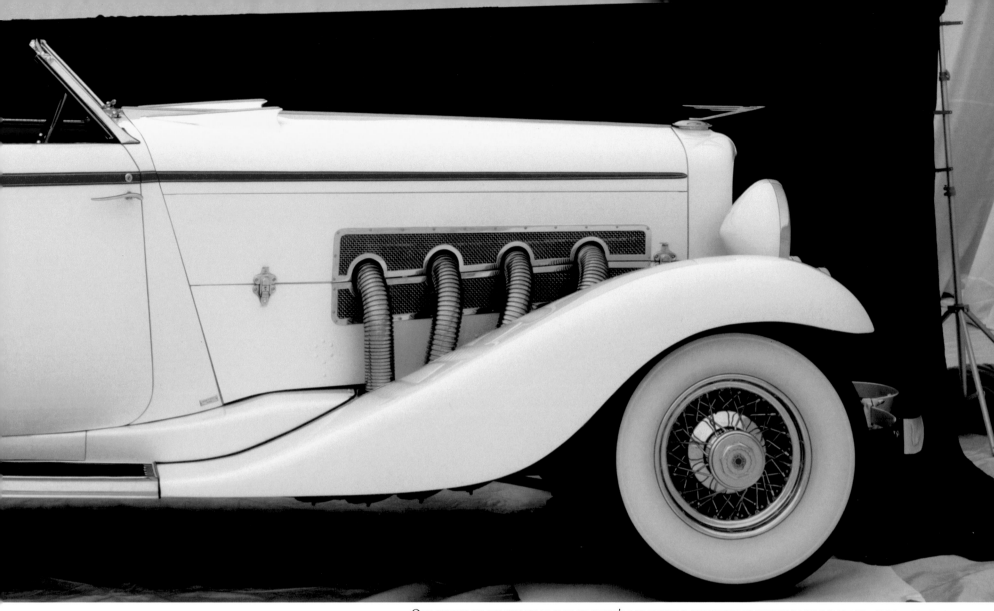

OUR STUDIO PHOTO SHOOT OF CLARKE GABLE'S DUESENBERG CONVERTIBLE, IN WHICH HE ROMANCED CAROLE LOMBARD.

WINDSHIELD VIEW OF THE FREEWAY

MURAL VIEW OF THE FREEWAY

Frank Gehry's Walt Disney Concert Hall
(Before and After)

FLOWER AND JEFFERSON C. 1972

144

MARLBORO MAN AND PEDESTRIAN
AVOIDING THE CAMERA
Wilshire Center

RUSCHA-ESQUE BOULEVARD AND FOG
From the Getty Museum

LOS ANGELES IS ENTERING A CULTURAL GOLDEN AGE, with local museums able to host world-class exhibits on a regular basis.

The privately run J. Paul Getty Center's virtually unlimited budget has allowed the acquisition of fantastic artistic treasures displayed in a building, designed by Richard Meier, high in the hills overlooking West LA. The new Disney Concert Hall in the heart of Los Angeles is a stunning example of futuristic architecture come to life, fanning hopes for a renaissance in the perennially rundown urban core of the city.

There is a darker side to the LA art scene, though. According to Mike Davis, author of *City of Quartz*, "The boom in public art and cultural monumentality has gone hand-in-hand with a culture depression in most of the inner city... ."

What the schools need is a return to art and music education, and to teach the kids to use computers creatively, so that they can all make their own web pages and blogs, and function productively in the future.
                                –Kathleen Goodwin

HENRY PERRY ROLLERBLADING
Venice Beach

SECURITY GUARD
Disneyland

JUGGLING BOWLING BALLS

QUEEN MARY

BABYLAND
Forest Lawn Cemetery

146

MAN IN CHICKEN SUIT
Santa Monica

GAS CHAMBER RESTAURANT
Orange County

Sand Volleyball Spike
Santa Monica

Barbara Kruger Installation
Temporary Contemporary Museum

MONORAIL CAR AND SNOWY MATTERHORN
Disneyland

ARCO MICROWAVE CHRISTMAS

MONKEY RINGS
Muscle Beach

PLANE TAKES OFF - FROM THE FREEWAY!
Harbor Freeway at the L.A. Airport

Downtown Gin Mill

Monks and Muscle Car

Los Angeles River

High-rise Lobby with
Long Shadows

151

Chapter 9

Beach Culture

Do you love me, do you surfer girl?

–Brian Wilson

The essence of California is inextricably intertwined with its beaches—the lightheartedness of the surf with the danger of the undertow.

SURFING AT RODEO BEACH
Marin

PARASAILING
San Diego

FISHEYE OF SANTA CRUZ
ROLLER COASTER TRACK

WITH ITS LONG COAST LINE, CALIFORNIA HAS INNUMERABLE BEACHES. Some–particularly those in Northern California–are foggy, windswept and cold, with hardly a person on them except a few fishing or surfing. In Southern California, cities have grown up around beaches jammed with people, complete with piers and promenades filled with joggers and dashing roller bladers. There are surfing competitions, beach volleyball tournaments (now an Olympic sport!), amusement parks, and junk food stands serving up corn dogs and cotton candy. Teenagers are fooling around, under the boardwalk, or under a blanket, because nobody's wearing very much clothing and everyone's having fun.

Perhaps the temperatures of the ocean affect the psyche of the people who live alongside it. In the south one can run spontaneously into its warm waters, while up north, it takes a considered decision of exhilarated frigidity or the ritual layering of Neoprene. For me, swimming in the ocean–north or south–is my nirvana. Although not a surfer myself, I can get a taste of it on my boogie board.

Within minutes of being on a beach, I relax, remembering the joy of life. It's the ocean, the large expanse of space, that makes me feel alive. One of the first things I do is check the water temperature. Like a lifeguard, I look for the undertow, the side washes. If swimming is not an option, I am happy to walk for miles along the beach looking for seals, porpoises, whales, treasures in the sand.

If I'm going to swim, I like to lie in the sun in a sheltered spot away from the ocean breezes until I get really warm and then I run in. For many years, if the water was cold, I went in slowly and painfully, but now I go in quickly and it's a thrill. The moment of putting my head in the water is the ultimate feeling of renewal. I can't help wondering–is this is how the ritual of baptism began?

Surfing pervades the Californian culture. In the sea, surfers must make a decision to go with the flow when they commit to riding a wave. If they are surfing at a place like the notorious Mavericks near Half Moon Bay, where the waves can be more than fifty feet high, their lives are at stake. The willingness to challenge

the sea has fostered the legend of the easygoing Californian who manages to survive the ocean at its most violent.

From the 60s, surfing was at the forefront of youth culture. As kids, we identified with the Beach Boys. We envied the California accents, the look of healthy athletic bodies, sun-bleached hair, surfing clothes, cars like Mustang convertibles and the woodies laden with surfboards. Surfing became an identity even adopted by people who can't actually surf but are drawn to the feeling of freedom, of youth, and the heroics of taking a wave. This is the land of the lifeguard and the beach bunny, the beach cottage and the body builder. From the 1959 film *Gidget* to the popular "jiggle" TV shows like *Baywatch* in the 90s, California is portrayed as a sand- and sun-fueled party state. Sam George wrote in *Surfer Magazine*: "If not for that pervasive Gidget myth, American youth would have missed one of the most potent archetypes available in the early 1960s–a rebellion based not on angst or anger, but on joy."

–Kathleen Goodwin

Santa Cruz Boardwalk

PADDLE BALL
Ventura

ARIEL BRAVES A WAVE
Santa Cruz

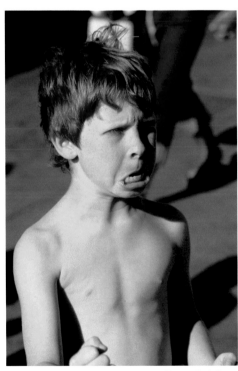

KUNG FU MOVE
Santa Cruz

THE BIG DIPPER ROLLER
COASTER
Santa Cruz Boardwalk

CO-ED SEMI-NUDE VOLLEYBALL
Black's Beach, Pacifica

DANIELLE SUNBATHING
Santa Cruz

Couple Kissing
Half Moon Bay

THE AUTHOR TAKES A WAVE
Point Reyes National Seashore

LET'S GO TO THE BEACH!

I often boogie board in Point Reyes National Seashore, near where we live. Here, the water is cold, so I have to wear a wet-suit that combines both thick and thin Neoprene for maximum protection and flexibility. I also wear booties and gloves. I used to wear a Neoprene hood as well, but now I prefer to have my head free. To catch a wave, I walk out to where the waves are breaking and if they are not too big, judge the break, trying to take one at just the right moment. Nothing beats the thrill of flying atop the curve of a wave to the shore. If I'm nervous about a bigger wave, I catch the white water after the break, and the force of the surf carries me in effortlessly. The length of time I surf generally depends on the temperature of the water—at 50 degrees, I can stay in about 30 minutes. Our local beaches are not set up for comfort (no hot showers), so if it's a cold day, I strip off my wet suit and immediately head home for a very hot shower.

–Kathleen Goodwin

KID HANGING OUT
Muscle Beach

Chapter 10

The Hippies

If someone thinks that love and peace is a cliche
that must have been left behind in the Sixties, that's
his problem. Love and peace are eternal.

–*John Lennon*

Dancing Hippie Family at Concert, 1969
Eucalyptus Grove, UC Berkeley Campus

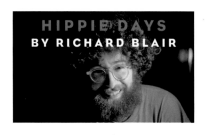

HIPPIE DAYS
BY RICHARD BLAIR

IT SEEMED WE WERE THE PIONEERS OF THE FUTURE, LIVING IN COMMUNES, EATING ORGANIC FOOD, GOING BACK TO THE LAND TO LIVE AS INDEPENDENTLY AS POSSIBLE. Was it our imagination or were we having more fun than any of the people we saw around us? The hippie movement was more than just a simple retreat from the modern world—it also changed society in many ways, small and large. People who had been determinedly climbing the corporate ladder suddenly quit their jobs, grew long hair and sought other ways to fulfill their dreams. Every aspect of life was questioned. Home births became the norm among hippies, with midwives attending the births accompanied by doctors who embraced the philosophy of letting nature do its work unassisted whenever possible.

With the baby boomers in their late teens and early twenties—peak years of physical beauty—the hippie era became one of unabashed sexuality. The advent of the Pill and other widely available birth control devices, freed young people from their fear of pregnancy, adding fuel to the fire of the sexual revolution. Although it's hard to believe now, sexually transmitted diseases were not a big problem: the plague of AIDS had yet to emerge, and herpes remained rare. The diseases of the time, syphilis and gonorrhea, were easily treated with antibiotics. Many of us suffered the vexations of crabs or scabies, of course, but these could be remedied with over-the-counter medications, followed by the cleansing ritual of boiling our clothes. All in all, this seemed a small enough price to pay for participating in the sexual revolution.

People had varying responses to this social scene. Some remained monogamous to a steady boyfriend or girlfriend and eventually married. Many

A HANDMADE WOOD STOVE
Mendocino

of these unions have lasted. The more sexually adventuresome enjoyed both male and female partners, attending orgies and wild parties. Some hippies took this new sexual freedom to impressive heights: I remember one female roommate who was "saving me for number one hundred." This unique combination of youth, the sexual revolution, and a lack of serious consequences helped fire the passions of hippies.

We liked to go camping in the national parks, and many kids met up in Yosemite around a campfire, perhaps their first summer away from home. The vehicles of choice for these trips were converted school buses, Volkswagen vans and "bugs", or classic American junkers, proudly painted in wild colors. We tore out the seats and put in blankets, foam pads and Indian fabrics.

Drugs were another defining part of being a hippie. First we tried marijuana while we were in school, and it seemed a very wicked and illegal act. For me, there were minute amounts available. I remember taking the tiny end of a joint and lighting it (while my head was inside a paper bag) to try to get high. Being stoned was a learned experience. For the neophyte, the effects of marijuana are very subtle, and many people could barely feel it. It is a drug that raises one's awareness but smoking too much can lead to a stupor or sleep.

LSD was the drug that really changed things. Just writing the initials on this keyboard seems dangerous. It is a very powerful drug. Mere micrograms—an infinitesimal amount—were enough to send a healthy person on an amazing, wild, and occasionally terrifying trip. Depending on the dose, the effects of LSD can last from eight to twelve hours. I believe that it breaks down the normal ability of the brain to keep non-survival perceptions and thoughts from overwhelming normal consciousness. To survive, animals must be totally aware of their environment, on the lookout for predators, and

Lothar and the Hand People
Eucalyptus Grove, UC Berkeley Campus

alert for danger. Humans' large brains need to be controlled, so there are built-in defenses against tripping out. One can't live in a constant state of profound revelations while experiencing amazing patterns and combinations of color, sound, and smells, when the main task is to survive. But in the post-industrial world, where much former work is now mechanized or computerized, and most wild predatory animals sadly confined to zoos, many hippies attempted to live stoned on acid (LSD) a great deal of the time. This stoned world meant the end of normal living in society. One could smoke the occasional joint and still go to school or hold down a job, but the all-encompassing effect of LSD was to live in a more spiritual, more loving world, without the trappings of conforming to a workday world. It seemed like a vast opening up, where the younger generation, with the wildness of youth, could totally re-invent the world and leave regular society "behind."

Not everyone who took acid could handle its power. People who were on the edge of mental illness could get worse, and the nightmares that everyone gets might become all too real—a terrifying experience. We were intrepid explorers, with the brazen courage of youth. Once, while tripping on acid, I was riding in a car on the way to Big Sur. I noticed that the breaking waves, seen from Highway One, had incredible rainbows. I remember trying to eat a turkey leg left over from a Thanksgiving dinner. Suddenly, I became aware that it was an actual creature's leg, and instead of looking like meat, it was a turkey's walking equipment. I remember thinking, "If I am eating his leg, shouldn't I try and use his energy, indeed his life, for some higher purpose?" I resolved to shoot some really good pictures of Big Sur.

I needed a drink to get the taste of this poor bird out of my mouth, so we stopped at a gas station on the intersection of Highways One and 101 near Castroville. I managed, somehow, to get lost at the Coke machine while my travel companions forgot all about me and went off to buy artichoke hearts. Every direction I looked I saw a freeway, and after a while I gave up trying to deal with it. I just sat down on a curb, figuring that I'd be arrested. In the midst of this confusion, my friends pulled up to retrieve me and off we went!

I took some beautiful images of Point Lobos, a park near Carmel, only to leave my Hasselblad (one of the world's most expensive cameras) on a rock there. Hours later, by a miracle, we found it still there. I remember

rubbing against some poison oak with my belly for the fun of it. By yet another miracle, I escaped the itch.

It was a wild and crazy time, with no going back. People who didn't become hippies seemed resentful, jealous or horrified by our lovemaking and drugs. Later, some became revisionists, using the media to portray us as losers, drug-dealing pushers. Uptight and angry history is now rewritten so our giant experiment in communal living, free love, and dropping out is seen as criminal activity. Writing truthfully about this time is dangerous because it scared the hell out of many people. When I see teenagers encumbered with shopping bags full of designer clothing from the malls, I think that these kids are perfect corporate robots, who live only to shop.

Communal living suffered no such hangups. Why work too much, when one could hang out with friends, saving money and sharing resources? Vegetarianism got a boost. Protein was obtained by combining various foods, like beans and rice. People took turns cooking and folks were always welcome to "crash", staying at each other's houses. Hitchhiking was the normal way to get round, and long hair and tie-dyed clothing were a passport to instant acceptance at parties, on the road, or at concerts. These hippie skills are much needed nowadays, because the earth can't support even today's population if everyone has every material thing they lust after. The future, whether we like it or

EXUBERANT HIPPIES AT GRATEFUL DEAD CONCERT
Angels Camp, Northern California

not, is a choice between a sharing culture or a war culture.

Concerts! Wow, what a great time! Working as a rock and roll photographer, I went to many shows: free concerts in Golden Gate Park, Bill Graham productions at Winterland and the Fillmore West, plus the Family Dog on the Great Highway in San Francisco. The music was amazing, the air heavy with marijuana smoke and incense, and the dancers spinning visions of beauty. Light shows projected mystical, colored patterns moving in time with the music, enhancing the effect of everything. Afterward, many people went home with each other for more personal lovemaking. San Francisco bands were in the forefront of the world music scene. Groups such as the Grateful Dead,

Psychedelic Harley
San Francisco

Quicksilver Messenger Service, the Jefferson Airplane (my fave), cross-pollinated with British bands like the Stones and Beatles, and for the first time a large white audience embraced great blues figures like B.B. King. Record companies suddenly began to recognize the vast buying power of the youth culture, as money flowed like great waterfalls of cash.

Hippie poster art was a visual interpretation of the psychedelic era. Hand-lettered and hard-to-decipher, this amazing artwork helped foster a secret and inclusive experience of truly belonging to another culture increasingly apart from the mainstream. The growing schism between "normal" society and this suddenly rebellious youth movement was made all the worse by increasingly oppressive drug laws passed by a government desperate to stem the tide of the hippie revolution. The lethal escalation of the Vietnam War furthered the profound disconnect between the hippies and regular society. The result is pictured in the next chapter, Counterculture, a reaction to the McCarthyism of the fifties and early sixties, the Vietnam war, the conformist corporate culture, and the environmental destruction spurred by development, pollution and greed.

In the end, the hippie vision of a pure and simple life was no match for the forces of ambition, conservatism, and the almighty dollar. The world seemed clear to the hippies: people were either hip, and thus fully tuned in to reality itself, or they were "pigs." This may seem a blunt and simplistic assessment, but when we look at our leaders today and the Iraq oil war, then think back to the motivations that led to the quagmire of Vietnam, perhaps the hippies, acting so instinctively and innocently, offered some answers that the world could use to be a more sharing and peaceful civilization.

–Richard Blair

CARLOS SANTANA
Altamont Rock Concert. 1969

THE ALTAMONT ROCK CONCERT

ALTAMONT WAS SUPPOSED TO BE THE WEST COAST VERSION OF WOODSTOCK, WHERE HALF A MILLION HIPPIES HAD HAD AN INCREDIBLY GOOD TIME THE YEAR BEFORE. Performing groups included the Jefferson Airplane and a very young Carlos Santana. Things got off to a good start, but two disastrous mistakes were made by Sam Waterford who, as road manager of the Rolling Stones, was the organizer of the concert. He paid the Hells Angels with a flatbed truck full of beer and had the stage constructed only two feet above the ground, thus providing an irresistible opportunity for concert goers to get close to the musicians. The Hells Angels, whose job was to keep the crowd back from the stage, became increasingly drunk as the day wore on and began to push back and fight the crowd physically. They got hold of some shortened cue sticks to beat the crowd and the vibe turned

GRACE SLICK AND JORMA KAUKONEN OF THE JEFFERSON AIRPLANE
Altamont

Altamont Audience at Sunrise

General Wastemoreland, Anti-Vietnam Activist, Working the Crowd

MORNING AT THE ALTAMONT CONCERT

ugly. At one point the drummer of the Jefferson Airplane had a tussle with one of the Hells Angels. I was photographing at the very front, between the crowd and the Hells Angels. The pressure of the crowd was so great that one of the rugged monitor speakers beside me suddenly crumpled as I turned to photograph a young boy being beaten up next to me. At this point, I decided that the event was totally horrible and since I felt in personal danger, I crawled under the stage, carefully avoiding the giant power cables. Climbing out the back, I was suddenly free of the violence and pushing. I sadly walked back to the highway and got a ride home. Later that night the violence turned fatal as a confrontation between an 18-year-old man, Meredith Hunter, and the Angels resulted in his being killed. At the trial, the Angel was acquitted, as Hunter was shown to have pointed a gun at the stage.

HELLS ANGEL
Altamont

VIOLENCE AT ALTAMONT

RENEE DANCING AT CASCADE CREEK
Mill Valley

KEN KESEY
Cody's Books, Berkeley

When people ask what my best work is, it's the bus. I thought you ought to be living your art, rather than stepping back and describing it.
—*Ken Kesey*

TWO ARTISTS WHO BECAME ICONIC FIGURES IN AMERICAN CULTURE EMERGED DURING THE HIPPIE ERA. **Ken Kesey,** the novelist who wrote *One Flew Over the Cuckoo's Nest* and *Sometimes A Great Notion*, became a Merry Prankster, traveling with the group in Further, the magic bus.

As the leader of the Grateful Dead, **Jerry Garcia** needs no introduction. The band's concerts were legendary from the early days in San Francisco when they played at Trips festivals, to huge all-day outdoor concerts where their followers would dance for hours during long, trance-like jam sessions. Sadly, both these amazing men have since passed on. Ken Kesey died in 2004 of liver cancer, and Jerry Garcia in 1995 from a heart attack exacerbated by sleep apnea. Their impact on this generation cannot be overstated.

KESEY'S SECOND VERSION OF THE FAMOUS MERRY PRANKSTER BUS
Cody's Books, Berkeley

JERRY GARCIA
Berkeley Keystone, c. 1976

Somebody has to do something, and it's
just incredibly pathetic that it has to be us.
–*Jerry Garcia*

Hippie Bus at Altamont

BEAR CAR, 1969

CHRISTOS ON TELEGRAPH

CLASSIC VW BUS
The Haight

FAT DOG'S CLOUD CAR, PAINTED BY CHRISTOS
Olmsted Point, Yosemite

TIE-DYED DANCER
Dead Show

Big Bud

Pot Greenhouse

Superhit

Bong

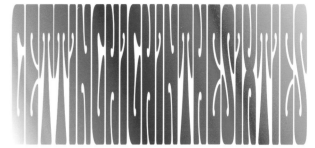

Hippie Pastime? (puzzle)

Naked Tripping Hippies

I wouldn't recommend sex, drugs or insanity for
everyone, but they've always worked for me.

–Hunter S. Thompson

TELEGRAPH AVE. LOVERS, 1970
Berkeley

MARSHA SANDERS, QUENTIN GOODRICH AND PUPPY
Parker Street Communal House, Berkeley, 1969

BAREFOOT BUS RIDER
Berkeley

DOME HOUSE AT ALTERNATIVE SCHOOL, 1975
Santa Cruz Mountains

BIKER WITH HOMEMADE DOG BOX
Berkeley

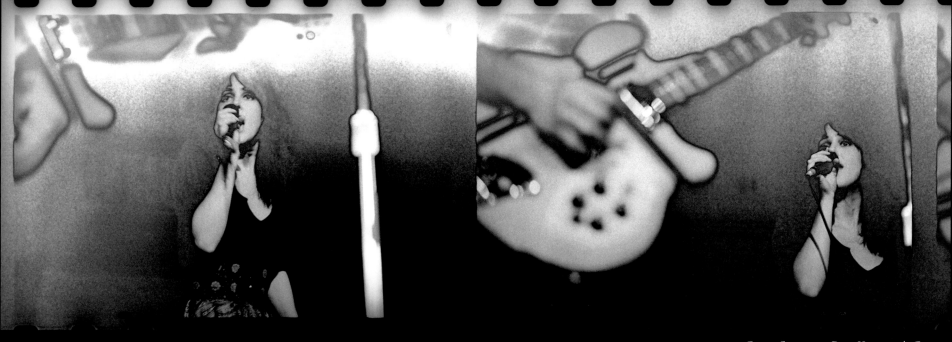

GRACE SLICK AND PAUL KANTNER'S GUITAR
Winterland (SF) New Year's Eve Concert, 1969

The negatives reversed when I inadvertently exposed the roll of film to light during the development process. As seemed typical of the time, my mistake turned positive when these unusual effects resulted. The image on the right was used on the record album, *Blows Against the Empire*, released in 1970, featuring the Jefferson Starship, Jerry Garcia, Graham Nash, Micky Hart, and David Crosby.

HIPPIE RELAXING FROM HITCHHIKING (WITH WHOLE EARTH CATALOG)

RENEE DANCING ON BLACK'S BEACH
San Mateo County

Chapter 11

Counter Culture

We didn't care if you were white, black, green, yellow or polka-dotted. We just wanted to know where your heart was.

—Bobby Seale

CONGA PLAYERS
Sproul Plaza, UC Berkeley

BERKELEY IS FAMOUS FOR ITS RADICAL POLITICS. From the 1950s, when a student party formed dedicated to ending nuclear testing, Cold War militarism, and capital punishment, to the current opposition to the Iraq War, Berkeley has been at the forefront of political protest.

In 1960, hundreds of Berkeley students took part in protests in San Francisco against the House Un-American Activities Committee (HUAC). Many were arrested. Police behavior brought out thousands of demonstrators the following day who decisively showed that they would not condone the hunting down of so-called communists.

Four years later, the U.C. Berkeley administration bowed to pressure from the politically conservative university regents, banning political recruiting and the distribution of pamphlets on or near the campus. Young people who had fought HUAC and had spent their summers signing up voters

in the South would not tolerate repression in their own backyard. The protests were much stronger than the administration or the regents had anticipated.

Led by civil rights activist Mario Savio, the Free Speech Movement was formed and had the support of many student political groups. Demonstrations grew and the graduate students went on strike. After Sproul Hall was occupied, the police arrested more than 770 students. The next day, 10,000 people massed to protest the arrests. Appalled by the police action, many of the Berkeley faculty posted bail for the students and supported the strike by refusing to hold classes. Ultimately, the student groups won the right to set up tables and recruit new

members, distribute political literature and sell political buttons and bumper stickers.

Fast on the heels of the Free Speech Movement came the anti-Vietnam War demonstrations, the rise of the Black Panther party, the Berkeley People's Park protest and the United Farm Worker strikes. In 1965 Lyndon Johnson sent troops to Vietnam, dividing the country between hawks and doves. For young men of draft age, the war was the ultimate injustice, and for many blacks and other minority kids, lack of an educational deferment meant being in combat. The Vietnam Day Committee held an early, large "teach-in" in May, 1965, with 20,000 people participating. The Oakland police stopped two attempts to march to the Oakland Army Base. The Hells Angels were on hand yelling, "Go back to Russia you fucking communists."

JONATHAN JACKSON'S FUNERAL, 1970
Oakland

ANTI-WAR DEMONSTRATOR WITH VIETCONG FLAG
San Francisco

DEMONSTRATION AFTER RODNEY KING VERDICT, 1992
Interstate 80, Berkeley

Just ten weeks later the Watts riots erupted in Los Angeles, the first of many uprisings of the sixties. They marked a change from the non-violent protests led by Martin Luther King in the south, to street riots. The next year Huey P. Newton and Bobby Seale started the Black Panthers, a militant group whose actions and speeches were inflammatory. Encouraged by the Black Power movement, others at the margins of society began to stand up for their rights. Mexican and Filipino farm workers went on strike against the grape growers in Delano, and a few years later, American Indians occupied Alcatraz Island, completing what was called "the Third World Movement."

Protests against racism continued to escalate through the late sixties

A HIGHWAY PATROL CAR BLOCKS THE FREEWAY
FOR THE PROTESTERS, 1992
Interstate 80, Berkeley

but the Vietnam War remained the primary focus of people's anger. A particular event stands out in the turbulent sixties as one of the most impassioned and violent. The University of California at Berkeley owned a large lot off Telegraph Avenue that was slated to become student dormitories. Telegraph Avenue was an exciting, congested area of hippies, students and street people, with retail shops, coffee houses and notably bookstores catering to them all. The idea that this large chunk of land would be much better used as a park took hold. People's Park was proclaimed and everybody really liked the idea except for the conservative regents, who responded by having a fence built around the land. The same day student leaders rallied people

ANTI-VIETNAM WAR DEMONSTRATION, 1969
Golden Gate Park, San Francisco

ANTI-IRAQ WAR DEMONSTRATION, 2005
Market Street, San Francisco

to "go down and take over the park." Large numbers responded and tore down the fence. A war started in Berkeley that day and night. The Alameda County sheriffs were called in to aid the Berkeley and campus police. James Rector, a bystander, was shot and killed by a sheriff's shotgun. Hundreds of people were injured. Governor Ronald Reagan sent in the National Guard. At one point, a National Guard helicopter flew over Berkeley bombing the protesters with tear gas. Strong winds blew the gas everywhere, radicalizing the entire city as their eyes burned.

Governor Ronald Reagan's popularity ironically soared among conservatives, who were very much in favor of the Vietnam War at the time. His cowboy approach helped propel him to the White House. It is worth pointing out that few of his supporters will now admit to their pro-Vietnam war beliefs, given the failure of the war and the fact that the dreaded communist domino effect never materialized.

Gays and lesbians were among many marginalized groups energized and inspired by the protests of the six-ties. The Stonewall riots in New York City in 1969 marked the first time that gays stood their ground and physically fought back against a police raid. Shocked by this sudden resistance, the embattled vice squad called for backup, but there was no response—their fellow police officers thought it must be a joke.

The rise of feminism in the 1970s came as a direct result of the counterculture encouraging people to fight for their rights. The disabled community, long ignored by all but their families, made its voice heard, and Berkeley is now proud to support organizations that supply customized wheelchairs and make sure that the city is accessible for disabled people. Sometimes the splinter groups of the era went crazy. The Symbionese Liberation Army assassinated the Oakland school chief, Marcus Foster, kidnapped Patty Hearst, then went on a bank robbing rampage that ended when most of the group was killed in a gun battle with police in Los Angeles. Typically, the establishment won the gun battles but the overall issues and freedoms fought for by the counterculture were won by the leftists through changing the country's way of thinking. Gay rights, women's rights, the end of the Vietnam War, the ecology movement and free speech—all advanced with the help of the protests in the sixties. America had come a long way from the passive conformist fifties, and while some were afraid of what we let out of the closet, most people found it liberating to live more freely. It takes constant vigilance to maintain a free and equitable society and we who are not rich should remember to demand our rights and a fair share of the economy.

—Thanks to Charles Wollenberg for information from his book, Berkeley, A City in History, *2002.*

FOOD NOT BOMBS PROTESTER, 1997
People's Park, Berkeley

POLICE LINE UP OUTSIDE FEDERAL BUILDING, IMMIGRATION RALLY, 2006
San Francisco

PROTESTS CONTINUE!

The unpopular war in Iraq has generated massive protests. Another big issue is immigrant rights, a subject every Californian experiences daily.

IRAQ WAR PROTEST, SAN FRANCISCO, 2002

IMMIGRATION AMNESTY RALLY, SAN FRANCISCO, 2006 (ALL PICTURES EXCEPT TOP RIGHT)

BERKELEY

I WALKED DOWN TELEGRAPH AVENUE IN BERKELEY FOR THE FIRST TIME IN 1970 AND FOR ME IT WAS LIKE COMING HOME. With my bell-bottom jeans and tie-dye T-shirt I fit right in. Not like in my hometown of Durban, South Africa, where such clothing made me stand out in any crowd. Here in Berkeley, this was the norm, and I liked it that way. The poet Julia Vinograd walked down the sidewalk blowing soap bubbles, street artists lined the pavements with colorful handcrafted wares, Hare Krishnas chanted, and street musicians played for the crowds. There was, however, a deeply felt intensity to the mood behind all those smiling faces.

The Civil Rights and Free Speech Movements of the 60s had galvanized Berkeley into a city of radical activists, attracting young people from all over

KPFA - A LONELY VOICE ON THE CORPORATE AIRWAVES
Berkeley

America and the world. Its citizens led the anti-Vietnam war protests and later the fight to stop nuclear weapons research at Lawrence Livermore Laboratory. Berkeley brought to the public's not always willing attention the abuses of large corporations, the effects of pollution, the rights of workers. It was in the forefront of the feminist movement. People were questioning every aspect of their lives. New environmental groups were established, while those already in existence became more politicized. The U.S. Government had to follow their constituents' lead. The influence of these times cannot be underestimated. I went back to South Africa and became a journalist focusing on the horrendous problems of apartheid and racism. Richard

KPFA, BERKELEY'S FREE-SPEECH RADIO STATION
Martin Luther King Way, Berkeley

Massive protests foiled an attempt by the Pacifica Foundation to control the content of KPFA and fire some of its commentators in 2000.

PROTEST BUTTONS ON SALE
Flea market, Berkeley

photographed riots and demonstrations on both the West and East coasts, spent the summer of 1967 in California, then moved here permanently in 1969.

Like so many other baby boomers, I rejected the corporate world. When I returned to California in 1974, I became a street artist, making feather jewelry. This was something totally new to me. I had never really worked with my hands before, nor had I ever sold anything. In many ways, I learned more about life during those two and a half years on Telegraph Avenue than I ever did at college or on my travels around the world. Everyday the street artists would either sign up for their assigned places on "The Ave" or take their chances in the lottery of the spaces not taken. I quickly learned the meaning of location—the west side of the street meant sun and people, the east side, shade and pollution. I had never before thought about the importance of four feet as opposed to five (very important if that is the size of your shop!). What made it fun were

the friends I made with the other artists, who were some of the most interesting and helpful people I have ever known.

During this time I lived in a well-established communal house, the "Frog House." Every night we sat down to a dinner cooked by one of the household. Generally eleven people, including four children, lived in our big house, but the large attic was often home to visitors. Throughout Berkeley, people were having similar experiences, learning firsthand that it was possible to enjoy most of life's pleasures if you were willing to share them.

Change is inevitable, however, and over time, the sunny character of Telegraph Avenue gradually soured. A hard-core street culture crept in. Many of the mentally ill people released from institutions by Ronald Reagan's policies came to live on this street. I finally gave up my prized street artist license after a very strange man angrily shook a raw leg of lamb in my face. I liked Fellini movies, but

did not care to live in one!

Perhaps it was an outcome of the marijuana munchies, but Berkeley gradually became the gourmet capital of California, if not America. Taking its cue from Alice Waters and her restaurant, Chez Panisse, Berkeley continues to astonish with the quality and variety of its restaurants and markets. Politically active Berkeleyites formed collectives that were not only politically correct but provided their customers with wonderful cheeses, croissants, quiches. One could eat exceptionally well and support the cause of the left! Now, organic, locally grown food at Farmer's Markets is the popular choice, without any modified genes, thank you.

Berkeley has also built model housing for many of its seniors, disabled, and homeless. Its tolerance for eccentrics is legendary, and the atmosphere of freedom and academic brilliance has attracted writers, poets, musicians and artists of every ilk.

–Kathleen Goodwin

TELEGRAPH AVE.
Berkeley

JULIA VINOGRAD
Berkeley's Street Poet

U.C. POLICE
People's Park

CAMPANILE
U.C. Berkeley

THE NIPPLE LADY
Telegraph Ave.

CULTS

CALIFORNIANS' INTEREST IN REMAKING THEMSELVES has led to the outgrowth of organizations that brainwash their followers with "love bombing" (repeatedly telling someone how wonderful he or she is, in a group session), sleep and food deprivation, and exploiting people when they are feeling depressed and vulnerable. The Moonies and the Krishnas pictured here are two of many such exploitative groups—another reason that those seeking their own path have to be extra careful of "friends."

We believe in religious freedom, but religious leaders can "cross the line" and cause tragedies such as Jonestown, where hundreds of followers, many Californians, had no choice but to kill themselves with poisoned punch at the command of their preacher, Jim Jones.

LOST GIRL
Telegraph Avenue, Berkeley

MOONIE FOLLOWER PROSELYTIZING
Shattuck Avenue, Berkeley

HARE KRISHNA CHANTING
Telegraph Avenue, Berkeley

Chapter 12

People of California

I'm not going to change the way I look or the way I feel to conform to anything. I've always been a freak. So I've been a freak all my life and I have to live with that, you know. I'm one of those people.

–John Lennon

KIDS WITH CAMERA
Twenty-Fourth Street, Oakland

PEOPLE OF CALIFORNIA

CALIFORNIA IS A LAND OF WILDLY DIVERSE ETHNIC GROUPS, ENCOMPASSING NATIONALITIES FROM EUROPE, ASIA, AFRICA AND THE AMERICAS. Recent years have seen a huge influx from our southern border, as legal and illegal immigrants from Mexico, Central, and South America come north in search of a better life. Although no part of the state has been left untouched, many of these newcomers have settled in the central and southern parts of the state. In certain districts of California cities, you'll have a hard time finding a single billboard or store sign in English.

In many ways, California represents the very essence of America itself, a land of immigrants bringing their energy, ambition, and vibrant cultures to a new world of opportunity. This tidal flow of immigration brings many problems as well, straining the resources and challenging the social and cultural structures of existing communities. Change is constant, and friction inevitable. Our great challenge will be to manage and absorb this influx fairly, for the betterment of all Californians, new and old.

The first European settlers were the Spanish padres, who established a series of missions and in the process, enslaved the native Indians. As more American settlers came West during the Gold Rush, many of the Mexican Land Grants were invalidated by these aggressive newcomers, who soon pushed for statehood. They succeeded in 1850, when California entered the union.

The Gold Rush and construction of the transcontinental railroad brought huge numbers of Chinese laborers to California, which they called "Gold Mountain." But the labor conditions they encountered were much akin to slavery, trapping them in contracts involving their ship fare and lodging that were nearly impossible to pay off. Nor was there a place in society for the Chinese, who were herded into ghettos in San Francisco, where they were confined during non-work hours.

A defining characteristic of people is that they are resistant to being held down, continually striving to regain their freedom and dignity. Over time, the Chinese in California succeeded, and now command a growing part of the economic power in the state.

Native Indians are still very much with us. Nowadays their tribal ties are getting stronger and they have an active interest in their own history and culture.

The Pacific Ocean is the largest feature of the planet. It is interesting to contemplate its huge edge, where the water meets the land, a common rim that stretches around the world, tying together the peoples and cultures of its coastline. Chinese, Japanese, Filipino, Pacific islanders, Russians, Central and South Americans, Australians, Indonesians—we are all connected by ships that navigate this huge expanse of ocean, bringing people, food, trade, and best of all, ideas, to all of the inhabitants. Hot spots on the shores of the Pacific—Hong Kong, Tokyo, Singapore, San Francisco, Sydney, and Los Angeles, for example—are blessed with natural harbors and climates favorable to the creation of great cities. Their markets, creativity, and cultures that develop spread around the world. In California, we are fortunate to be the recipient of all this *people energy* from abroad.

Computers, farming, genetic research, the rise of the automobile and the freeway, the movies and hippie culture —these are modern Californian exports. We enlarge, enhance, and project huge influences around the world by being on the forefront of innovation and change.

We cannot possibly do justice to all the different groups of people in California with a picture or even a mention in this book. I'm thinking, for example, of the people who came from the Indian subcontinent: when was their main immigration? Did they come recently, with the high-tech boom, or have they been here much longer, drawn by the opportunity of the Golden State? So many of our brightest thinkers were first schooled overseas.

A more complete portrait of Californians would be another book. In this chapter, we focused on images shot over the years, attempting to capture the spirit of brotherhood that is always there, if only one looks. California's history of racism—from the holocaust of the Indians to the exploitation of immigrant labor—is one that we should all work to put behind us. Please understand that we are not meaning to stereotype our subjects. We are trying to show the value—indeed, the necessity—of all of us living in relative harmony as individuals who are together defining the future.

TINY AND GIRLFRIEND, 1969
Telegraph Ave, Berkeley

Angry Cabbie in Friendly Cabs (I set him up with a dirty look, I'm afraid)
San Francisco

YOUNG GIRL WITH FACE PAINTING
Make-A-Circus, Oakland

YSENIA DANCING WITH BETO

Quinceañera

ADAM & EVE
Merced County Fair

Vivian Hanging Out

CHINESE COMPETITORS
Los Angeles

All Together Now!

Bev and Debbie Serving Garlic Spaghetti
Gilroy Garlic Festival

BLASTING FOR GOLD

These women are explosives experts. The truck behind them is filled with a high-power liquid explosive, a pearlescent white viscous fluid that they carefully pump into holes in the ground. The crater where they're working is the result of their previous efforts. This work is gender-specific: only women are allowed to set up and detonate the explosives, as men are not considered as careful or as safety-conscious. How this mining operation works is completely at odds with the way people think of miners and the Gold Rush. Survey crews dig core samples to determine the exact concentration of gold throughout the mine. The price of gold, or the need for the company to get a tax break, determines which area of the mine is worked.

After the explosive is loaded, the women set electric triggering devices. Everyone leaves the area and at 3 PM, there is a huge explosion. Operators (both female and male) then drive huge trucks of the broken rock to a big opening covered with a sorting mesh (to keep the largest rocks out) and dump their load. The hole is over a gigantic conveyor-belt system that transports the ore to grinding mills that reduce the rocks to mud. The mud is pumped into a chemical plant as big as a refinery, where the gold is painstakingly separated out. In the final stage, the gold is poured into ingots—bars of pure gold—like one would see in a James Bond movie. Visitors are not permitted to see this part of the process.

Owned and run by the Homestake Mining Company, this mine is about nine miles from Clear Lake, in Northern California. Because the mine is on a small mountain road, shipments of gold are never sent by armored truck. Instead, they are hidden in an ordinary car to lessen the risk of an ambush. In this small way, some aspects of the Old West still live on.

Women Blasting Crew Laying Fuse Cord

The Three O'Clock Explosion!

Gold!

LINE AT THE VIETNAMESE CATERING TRUCK
Peerless Lighting, Fourth Street, Berkeley

Many jobs in California are factory jobs—
punching the clock, taking breaks, pretty
much like a factory anywhere in the world.
In the picture above, lighting company
workers line up at the affectionately called
"roach coach," a catering truck that serves the
best Vietnamese-style egg rolls.

This worker is at a paint factory that I photographed for their annual report. I was shocked. The walls of the building were peeling because they hadn't been painted for years. The smell of solvent was overpowering, even though everywhere I looked huge industrial fans were blowing the chemicals out of the building and into the San Francisco Bay air. I wasn't allowed to use a flash in the building. My guide explained that a tiny spark could blow up the place. All of the lights and motors were specially shielded with double housings to avoid such sparks. I thought it would be interesting to photograph the paint being mixed in one of the giant mixers. I leaned forward with my camera to photograph the swirling chemicals. The guide grabbed my upper arm with a steely grip. "Never lean into a mixer," he said. "You'll pass out before you know it and fall in." Later he told me a story about two men who caught on fire in the resin department. They ran down to the nurse's station to get help only to catch the beds on fire. He said that they died later.

It was unbelievable to me that this factory could exist in the Bay Area. The attitude of the management toward pollution and worker safety was criminal.

WORKER AT PAINT FACTORY
San Francisco

DON'T GET THESE WORKING AT THE FACTORY
Santa Monica

STEVE WOZNIAK

Steve Wozniak: Co-founder of Apple Computer

Stephen Wozniak (born August 11, 1950) is a computer engineer turned philanthropist. His inventions and machines contributed enormously to the personal computer revolution of the 1970s.

Wozniak co-founded Apple Computer with Steve Jobs in 1976 and created the Apple I and Apple II computers in the mid-1970s. The Apple II became the best-selling computer of the 1970s and early 1980s; it was the first popular personal computer.

When I photographed Wozniak for *Computer Currents* in the late 1980s, my fellow journalists asked him many questions about the future of Apple and computing. At one point he turned to me and asked if I had any questions. "Just one", I said jokingly, "how much do you make?" He thought for a moment and replied "About $100,000 a day, after taxes and everything." That was a very impressive answer for a freelance photographer!

Later, his mother called me. She said that the cover image was her favorite photo of her son, so I sold her a print for twenty-five dollars.

Pharoah Sanders: Jazz Master

Pharoah Sanders was born on October 13, 1940 in Little Rock, Arkansas. The son of two musicians, he moved to Oakland after high school, studying art and music at Oakland Junior College. He became well known in the Bay Area, then moved to New York in 1962, where he played with Don Cherry, Billy Higgins and Sun Ra. In 1964, John Coltrane invited Sanders to sit in with his band, and soon he was playing regularly with the group. After Coltrane's death in 1967, Sanders played briefly with his widow, Alice Coltrane. Since the late 1960s, Pharoah Sanders has had his own band, recording extensively.

Superconductor with a Magnet Floating Above It
UC Berkeley

Radio Telescope and the Sierra
Owens Valley

Amazed by the Screen
Computer Currents Cover

California owes much of its lead in computer technology to the foresight of the founders of Stanford University, Leland and Jane Stanford, who decreed that none of the 8,000 acres they had donated for the university grounds could ever be sold. To fund the construction of new buildings, the university leased land to industry. The Stanford Industrial Park was founded in the 1950s–limited to high-technology companies.

A few years earlier, in 1946, a group of business executives had joined the university to create the Stanford Research Institute (SRI), a West Coast center of innovation modeled after the renowned Bell Labs in the East.

The stage was set for California to bring computer technology to the masses.

The University of California (UC) is a world-famous university system, with ten campuses spread throughout the state. Students from all over the world compete to attend one of these campuses, knowing that a degree from UC can be their ticket to a successful future. Although lacking the prestige of the Ivy League, UC's influence is considerably more profound due to the sheer number of students involved. Approximately 150,000 students are presently enrolled in UC, with admissions expected to increase to 210,000 in the next few years.

California has produced more than 90 Nobel Laureates, 40 associated with UC, 31 from the California Institute of Technology (Caltech), 23 from Stanford and one from the University of Southern California. Caltech is a small, independent university particularly famous for its physics department. Albert Einstein and Niels Bohr were visiting scholars in the 1930s.

California is also foremost in the field of genetics and DNA technology. In 1972 Paul Berg of Stanford University created the first recombinant DNA molecules by combining the DNA of two different organisms. In 2004 Californian voters authorized a $3 billion bond to fund stem cell research.

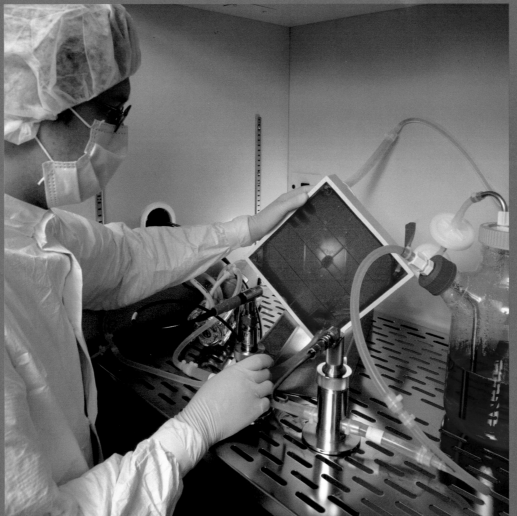

GENETIC ENGINEERING FOR A HEMOPHILIAC TREATMENT
California leads the world in DNA research

INMATES, SAN QUENTIN

California is a bad place to be busted: three strikes and you're out, with a mandatory twenty-five-year to life prison sentence after three felony convictions. Except for South Africa, the Golden State has a larger percentage of its citizens locked behind bars than any country on Earth. This is a sad and sick situation. Every year the schools fail many of our kids, leaving them suitable only for menial job, with a predictable result—they cast their bets on a life of crime. The ultimate penal horror is Pelican Bay, home to the most violent inmates, held underground 24 hours a day, for years on end. The prospect of entering this gulag, even as a photographer, was too much for me, so I shot this photo from a nearby road. From there, the maximum-security prison looked no more ominous than a community college, utterly peaceful above ground. With all the inmates and prison personnel kept below ground, there wasn't even a guard at the gate. The banality of evil never seemed so creepy.

When my friend David Vassar was filming inside San Quentin for the television show "Unsolved Mysteries," I went along as the still photographer. The day was beautiful, but the instructions from the prison seemed foreboding: "Don't wear blue, and don't run," the guard explained. "If there's a problem, we shoot the blue things." He then warned us that if we were taken hostage by the prisoners, there would be no bargaining for our release.

San Quentin reminded me of a lousy high school in a tough neighborhood. The prisoners shown here signed model releases for the photo shoot. I wish them well, and thank them for helping me show what life in prison is like.

PELICAN BAY
The inmates are underground

GUARD WITH RIFLE

SAN QUENTIN CELL BLOCK AT NIGHT (2)

TATTOOED INMATE

DRUMMERS
Santa Barbara

DRUM CIRCLE
Santa Barbara

DANCER
Santa Barbara

Pre-game Party on a RV Roof
Oakland Coliseum

JOGGER AND HOMELESS PACK RAT
Santa Monica

FIRE BREATHER, MAKE-A-CIRCUS
Oakland

HOMELESS
San Francisco

Chapter 13

California Country

Ninety-nine percent of the world's lovers are not with their
first choice. That's what makes the jukebox play.

–Willie Nelson

Grazing Horses and Wildflowers
Gorman

Carl Weatherford with Lariat
Bear Valley Ranch, near Wilber Springs
We went to the Bear Valley to photograph the wildflowers. We saw a perfectly outfitted cowboy roping steers. Later we learned his name from a fellow cowboy. The barn on the opposite page is on the same ranch, which was resplendent with blossoms.

A LARGE PERCENTAGE OF CALIFORNIA IS RURAL, WITH COUNTRY TOWNS, FARMS, AND PLENTY OF LAND THAT IS TOO DRY OR TOO STEEP TO CULTIVATE. It is home to a largely unknown population in California, the rural folk. Many embrace cowboy roots. Most are religious and conservative in their political leanings. Many are poor. They live in areas with little economic growth, not part of the huge California economy of high tech, tourism, Hollywood, and large-scale farming. Many are retired. Their housing is less regulated by strict building codes and range from beautiful old farmhouses, Victorians and period classics to mobile homes and funky shacks.

When you travel in California, the spaces between the cities, national parks and other attractions is the land of rural California. It is an important part of the state. It also is a link to California's past, because the lack of development—which transforms and rewrites the landscape in ever-uglier manifestations of suburbia and strip malls—is its saving grace. It is California in a preserved and ornery state.   —Richard Blair

RODEO!

RODEO COWBOY WITH BUCKING BULL
Guerneville

PRACTISING ROPING
Golden Gate Fields Parking Lot

RODEO CHIMP, CLOWN AND COWGIRLS
Guerneville

RUSTED FORD TRUCK PANEL
Marshall

SIGN ON GATE
Feather River Canyon

ABANDONED DRIVE-IN
WITH PLOWED FIELD
Central Valley

INDEPENDENCE DAY
Dutch Flat

Poodle in RV

The World's Funkiest Trailer
Randburg

Camp Under Bridge
Tracy

Dreamy Pickup Seat
Half Moon Bay

223

Chapter 14

The Corners of California

There is science, logic, reason; there is thought verified by experience.
And then there is California.

–Edward Abbey

FENCE AND BIRD
U.S.–Mexican Border
A fence not by Christo...

I DIDN'T REALIZE JUST HOW BIG AND HOW DIVERSE CALIFORNIA WAS UNTIL I DECIDED TO VISIT THE FOUR CORNERS OF THE STATE.

The northwest end of the state is just past Crescent City–wet, lush, a land of redwoods, fishing and wild rivers, like the Smith River near the Oregon border. The next trip was to the northeast corner, near the town of Cedarville on the edge of the Great Basin, with alkali lakes, fields of green alfalfa, and Cascade-type mountains.

The southwest corner was more difficult.

The congested freeways of Los Angeles blocked easy access to the south. We finally managed to get there and hiked to the border of Mexico and California, where an ominous wall marches into the surf.

It was an easy ride over to the southeast corner, where the border follows what is left of the mighty Colorado River. Water diversions have left only a small river, and the surrounding area are mostly sand dunes and desert.

I had never heard of anyone making such

a trip to see the corners of California, and I am really glad I did. Each area was so different from the others that it was like visiting four separate countries. Californians are able to live in different worlds here, all within one state.

I remember taking my dog to these wildly different ecosystems, one week the Sierra, the next the desert, another weekend the big city and I thought, this dog is a real expert among dogs, he has seen it all. I don't know if it improved him, but I felt that he was sophisticated

N

W

E

S

FOUR CORNERS OF CALIFORNIA

upper left: The Pacific Ocean coast near the northwest

upper right: A farm near the northeast

lower left: A Border Patrol sentry on the southwest

lower right: The end of the Colorado River at the southeast

and worldly wise. The point remains, there is no other state in America where changes in landscape are so huge.

Think of a Texan and sagebrush comes to mind, but picture a Californian and one thinks of what? Surfer, cowboy, jazz musician, farmer, scientist, backpacker, suburbanite, actress, hippie–the list could be endless.

Take a look at the four corners of the state and think about what they mean in terms of your perceptions of the state of California. In the southeast they are trying to keep Mexicans out. In the northeast, they are desperate for more people. At Crescent City in the Northwest we send the most violent people to Pelican Bay State Prison while and in the southeast we take what is left of the Rocky Mountain's water and convert it to irrigation for crops in the Imperial Valley, creating a man-made oasis and robbing Mexico.

One tries to think of the state in terms of good or bad, but the reality of California goes far beyond those simple concepts. As you will discover in your travels here, this is a place only the gods could fathom.

–Richard Blair

BLACKBIRD, ALFALFA FIELDS, ALKALI LAKE BED
Surprise Valley, Modoc County

CASTLE CRAGS

FISHING CREW, CRESCENT CITY

REDWOOD CIRCLE

PAPERMILL CREEK , DAWN

MT. SHASTA ENGULFED IN A STORM THAT TRAPPED CLIMBERS

HERD OF DEER

COYOTE PUPS IN IRRIGATION PIPE

CATTLE AND ALKALI LAKE

MIDDLE ALKALI LAKE
KATHLEEN GOODWIN

OLD DESERT CAR
Surprise Valley

MEXICAN LIGHTHOUSE
US-Mexican border

NORTH AND SOUTH OF THE BORDER

MEXICAN FAMILY AND THE BORDER FENCE

The southwestern corner is dominated by the politics of the U.S.–Mexican border. The black metal wall, weirdly reminiscent of Christo's *Running Fence,* serves to prevent immigration, while California is completely dependent on Mexican workers for its economic well being.

At the southeastern corner is a huge Indian casino; nearby, miles of sand dunes are being torn up by desert-destroying off-roaders. It's also the end of the mighty Colorado River, the last of its waters sucked up by a canal to irrigate the Imperial Valley. When this canal broke in 1905 the Salton Sea resulted. No water from the river reaches Mexico, where people now live in the dry stream bed. Occasionally, after major rains, not all the water is diverted and Mexican villages have been tragically flooded.

Both the southwest and southeast corners of the state are degraded landscapes.

WILDFLOWERS
Tijuana Estuary State Park

ALGODONES DUNES

OCOTILLO CACTUS

QUECHAN CASINO
Yuma, Arizona-California Border

MAN WITH WATER BOTTLE
Colorado River

DIRT BIKE RIDER
Imperial Sand Dunes Recreation Area

Chapter 15

California Wine

Wine to me is passion. It's family and friends. It's warmth of heart and generosity of spirit. Wine is art. It's culture. It's the essence of civilization and the art of living.

–Robert Mondavi

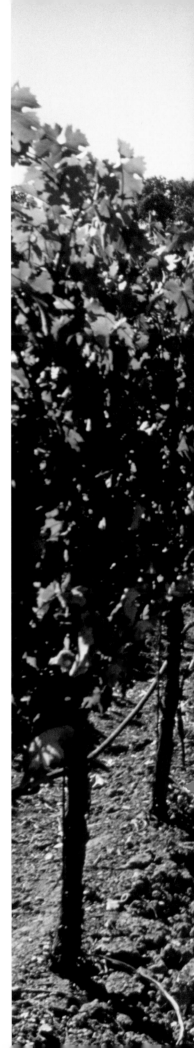

Hartwell Winery

CALIFORNIA VINEYARD HISTORY

THE FIRST WINE GRAPES GROWN IN CALIFORNIA WERE PLANTED IN 1769 BY THE FRANCISCAN PRIEST, FATHER JUNIPERO SERRA, FOR THE MISSION AT SAN JUAN CAPISTRANO. The grape vines are believed to have come from the so-called mission grapes, used in Mexico by the Catholic Church for the celebration of the Roman Mass. Many years later, the strict requirement of wine for this ceremony actually saved the California wine industry during Prohibition.

In Mexico in 1525, the Governor of Mexico, Hernando Cortez, ordered grapes to be planted. These were so successful that in 1595 the King of Spain forbade new vine planting in Mexico, retaining the commercial market in the colony for the Spanish vintners for the next 150 years.

European vines were first planted in Los Angeles in 1833. During the 1850s and 1860s, a Hungarian soldier and entrepreneur known as "Count" Agoston Harazsthy became the father of the modern Californian wine industry by importing cuttings of 300 different grape varieties from 165 of the best European vineyards. He founded the Buena Vista Winery in Sonoma in 1857, now a California Historic Landmark.

A problem in the early vineyards was the organism *phylloxera*, known as "root louse," which was endemic to American soil and destroyed the roots of the European wine vines. The tough, fibrous root bark of American vines prevented *phylloxera* from penetrating and damaging the plants, but the European grapes lacked this natural resistance. The use of pesticides in the vineyards only delayed the attack. In 1863, *phylloxera* spread to Britain when species of the native American grapes were taken to the Botanical Gardens in London. It took only two years for *phylloxera* to jump over to Europe, where it killed most of the wine vines.

Eventually, grape producers found that grafting the European vines to American root stock produced a plant resistant to root louse without affecting the taste of the grapes. Only vines that had the grafted American root stock survived, so many varieties of grape that were not commercially viable became extinct.

While the European vineyards were experiencing this crisis, the American wine industry flourished. The crown jewel was the Napa Valley, named by the Wappo Indians, its first residents. "Napa" means land of plenty. By 1889, there were more than 140 wineries in Napa Valley, but a new catastrophe threatened.

At the turn of the 20th century many American saloons were places where drinking to excess was the norm and gambling and prostitution thrived. The temperance movement of reformers against alcohol consumption grew stronger. Carrie Nation, with fellow reformers, attacked caskets of whiskey, hatchets in hand. In 1920, the 18th Amendment prohibited the manufacture, sale, and transport of alcohol, with the notable exception of sacramental wine used in the church. Certain savvy Napa Valley vintners, particularly Georges de Latour of the Beaulieu Vineyard, survived Prohibition by producing sacramental wine.

The California wine industry was reinvented after the repeal of Prohibition in 1933. A major figure was a young Russian-born émigré, André Tchelistcheff, whom de Latour found in 1938 working in Paris at the Institut National Agronomique. De Latour invited Tchelistcheff to work with him in California. Tchelistcheff introduced many innovations to Napa Valley and had a profound influence on its wine industry until his death in 1994. Tchelistcheff modestly thought James Daniel Jr. of the Gustave Niebaum estate was Napa's greatest wine maker. Daniel's 1941 Cabernet Sauvignon is still considered one of the finest wines ever produced in California.

The wine world was rocked in 1976 when, at a blind tasting in Paris, nine French experts gave a California wine the highest ranking. Five years later, *New York Times* wine critic Terry Robards wrote, "American wines are often challenging French wines in tasting competitions these days, and the results often suggest that certain carefully chosen California wine are superior to the best that France can offer." These competitions are good for the wine drinker. May all wines, French, American, or from the other great vineyards of the world, continue to evolve and improve! ***Salude, Sante, Cheers!!!***

GRAPE STOCK AND MUSTARD
Carnernos

KNIFE USED TO PICK GRAPES

236

HARTWELL WINERY
all photographs this page

Hartwell Winery

Hartwell Winery

CABERNET SAUVIGNON GRAPE LEAVES

SUNSET, NAPA VALLEY
Yountville

Irrigation

Chateau Souverain

WINE: SCIENCE AND MYTHS

The wine industry in California has steadily improved over the years, the result of a careful study of the science of wine making. The front of a winery may look like a château, but behind this exterior are stainless steel vats whose contents are minutely studied. Through centuries of winemaking, the French gleaned techniques that improved the quality of their wines. Lacking that long history of hard-won knowledge, Californians went to the laboratories to analyze wine production scientifically. Among their findings was that off-flavors in wine can develop through excess heat during fermentation, so now the stainless steel fermentation tanks are built to regulate the temperature strictly. The wine is later put into French oak barrels, as the flavor of the oak adds to the complexity of the wine. A new trend is to add wood chips to the wine within the jacketed steel vats.

Winemakers have come to realize that the health and vigor of their grapes have a strong effect on the quality of the wine. Many employ principles of organic grape growing and the quasi-mystical science of biodynamics to create the healthiest and most vibrant grape juice. Biodynamic agriculture is a holistic regimen wherein soil is nurtured by adding animal and vegetable matter to strengthen it, along with various homeopathic herbal and mineral preparations to help the soil maximize light and heat for photosynthesis. The entire process–planting vines, harvesting grapes, and bottling the wine–is performed in accordance with the positions of the planets and lunar phases. Using these and other innovative techniques, grape growers claim to achieve tremendous amounts of sugar in the grape before harvest, resulting in a higher alcohol content for the finished wine. Some purists complain that the flavors of such wine are too "hot," but in the highly subjective arena of wine tasting, there is only one hard and fast rule: "De gustibus non est disputandum." ("There's no accounting for taste.") Perhaps it is the biodynamic methods that produce the results or it could be the close attention these grape growers pay to their crops.

The University of California at Davis and Fresno State University both have wine research centers. UC Davis teaches winemaking as an exacting science in the laboratory, while Fresno State favors a more hands-on approach–their students grow and press the grapes, then bottle the wine. They sell 25,000 cases each year under their own label.

Scientists are researching using genetically modified yeast in the winemaking process. The product is controversial–Europeans frown on importing GMO foods, and the organic wine movement is aghast, but some say it improves the wine and the yeast itself is not found in the end product.

California produces extraordinary wine. Blind tastings bear this out. The hard work of all the people involved in the wine industry now gives us some of the best wines in the world. We can all toast to that!

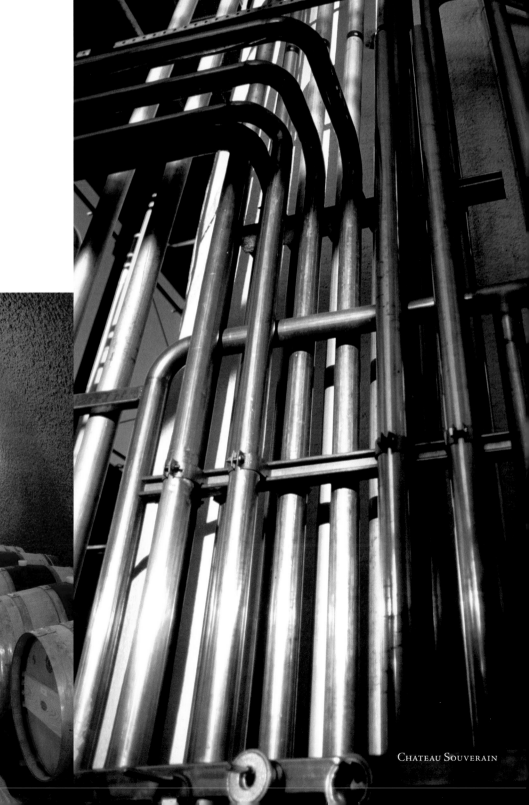

HARTWELL CAVE

CHATEAU SOUVERAIN

OLD WOODCUT OF BUENA VISTA WINERY
This woodcut of workers tending the Buena Vista vineyards was published in an early guidebook to California. Artists were sent to California and their sketches used by woodcarver engravers in the East who carved the scenes into the end grain of wood blocks, which were then inked in a printing press.

GRAPE LEAVES TURNING GOLD
Yountville

Oak Barrels

LOOKING UP THE VALLEY FROM OAKVILLE ROAD
Napa Valley

SCREAMING EAGLE VINEYARDS IN NAPA VALLEY

AN AMERICAN ARI$TOCRACY

AGRICULTURAL LAND IN NAPA VALLEY IS A SCARCE AND HIGHLY PRIZED COMMODITY. Housing prices in the valley have reached astronomical heights–$20 million or more for an estate–which has transformed the sleepy Napa Valley into one of the premier localities where rich people congregate. Signs of wealth are everywhere–stunning chateaus perched on hills overlooking vineyards for miles in all directions, the elaborately constructed gates and stone walls, manicured gardens and gourmet delicatessens like Dean & DeLuca. The renowned French Laundry restaurant features tiny portions of exquisitely prepared food. It's eating as a form of worship. Rolls Royces and Ferraris cruise the backroads.

The valley abounds with celebrities. Robert Redford,

SHAMROCK AT POETRY INN, NAPA VALLEY

Joe Montana, Robin Williams, Francis Ford Coppola and Boz Scaggs all have wineries. Today, it costs at least $5 million to build a winery, not counting the cost of the land! The Napa Wine Auction sells tickets for $7,500 to its charity auction, where the high bid for a Screaming Eagle Cabernet set the record for a cult wine–a six-liter bottle of 1992 Cabernet sold for $500,000. Some of the auction money is used to build farmworker housing centers. A 60-bed center, on land donated by Joseph Phelps, will be the Cadillac of farmworker housing. At $3 million, it will cost $50,000 a bed, and workers will pay $14 per day for room and board.

Napa is a place for living grandly–and being generous with what good soil, sun and noble grapes bring!

OPUS ONE
Napa Valley

PAOLETTI ESTATES WINERY
Silverado Trail, Napa Valley

NAPA VALLEY RURAL ARCHITECTURE

CULINARY INSTITUTE OF AMERICA FOUNTAIN

Chapter 16

Agriculture

In the span of my own lifetime I observed such wondrous progress in plant evolution that I look forward optimistically to a healthy, happy world.

—*Luther Burbank*

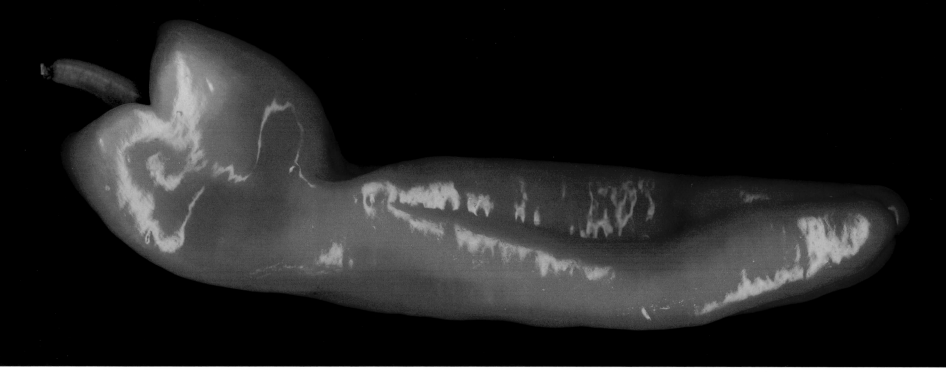

California puts more food on America's dining tables than any other state. At least a third of the food grown in the United States comes from the Golden State.

However, it doesn't come easily. Farm labor is backbreaking work, mostly performed by Latinos without citizenship. Many of the farms in California are huge agribusinesses growing mono-crops that have to be heavily fertilized and sprayed with pesticides to survive. As a result, farm workers are getting sick. Scientists are finding that pesticides drifting in the winds from the Central Valley are poisoning lakes in the High Sierra, which particularly affects frogs and trees.

While there are large resources of water from the Sierra and even the Colorado River, cities, real estate developers and agriculture all compete for it. Environmentalists have entered the fray to ensure that wildlife, too, has enough clean water to survive. The aquifers are being drained and the water tables are dropping.

Genetically modified organisms are developed and sold with insufficient testing. And how can a company patent a life form? Are we going to be eating Monsanto cow-pigs? It bothers us that many genetically modified products are not labeled as such.

Nevertheless, when we drive through the Central Valley we always sense the positive energy—there is no denying that growing all that food is a miracle of agriculture. The people who work so hard to make it happen—from the bankers and mechanics to the farmers and truckers—are proud that they create so much abundance.

Anybody who has seen poverty in the Third World knows the importance of this agricultural miracle. We hope that the impossibly complex combinations of water wars, farm subsidies, international commerce and labor disputes will not ruin California's bounty in the future.

There are many challenges ahead. Farmland is not as valuable as developed land. People will pay more for land devoted to housing, shopping centers and other suburban and urban projects. Because California is such a desirable place to live and work, housing prices are astronomical. People drive for hours to work every day so that they can live in their own home. More than 100,000 acres of farmland are lost every year.

When I first came to California, I was hanging out with kids who had grown up around Half Moon Bay. I visited a farm stand there where my friend, Quentin, knew the farmer. He gave us some avocados. I had never seen one before. My friends were in ecstasy. They peeled off the skin, dumped some salt on the meat, and scarfed it down. What a strange treat for a New York kid. Later I tried my first artichoke. Peeling the petals one by one, dipping them in melted butter, and then working my way down to the heart was a cosmic experience for a young urbanite. Since then, I have always appreciated the amazing quality and variety of California fruits and vegetables.

When I think how important it is to feed everyone, yet balance water policy, environmental protection and labor standards, I shudder over the dismal state of the political process that attempts to achieve that equilibrium. It seems as though the only people at the table who influence policy have paid big bucks to be there.

California can continue to feed so many only if all the stakeholders—the farmers, their workers, the organic movement, the consumers and the voters of the state—continue to help agriculture improve. Through what we buy in the market, and how we vote, we can keep our state healthy and productive.   –Richard Blair

FLOWERING ALMOND ORCHARD
Kern County

SHEEP RETURNING TO THE BARN
Sonoma County near Occidental

LOCAL, ORGANIC & SUSTAINABLE AGRICULTURE

WHY LOCAL?

On average, American farmers receive less than twenty cents per dollar for their products. The majority of our food dollar goes to middlemen, such as food brokers, distributors, and retailers. By comparison, when we purchase locally produced food, a much higher return per dollar goes to the farmer. In the case of farmers markets for example, the farmer receives 100% of each dollar we spend. In addition, when we spend money in our community, it gets circulated an average of seven more times inside the community before it's finally spent outside. So,

when we buy locally grown produce, we are not only supporting our local farmer, we're also supporting the entire local economy. A healthy community is the result of millions of decisions made everyday by the people who live there, and it can be altered by every single choice we make – whether at the grocery store or how we treat our neighbors. So, the next time you go grocery shopping, ask yourself how much influence on your local food system and your local economy you want to have, and look for local and organic labels.

WHY ORGANIC?

Time and again, studies have documented the health benefits of organically grown food over non-organically grown food, and not just because of the absence of chemical pesticides and herbicides. Organically grown produce consistently tests higher than non-organically grown foods for vitamins, minerals, and other micro-nutrients, as well as showing much smaller amounts of nitrates, heavy metals and other contaminants. One of the main reasons for the nutritional discrepancy is that organic soil is much richer in minerals and micro-nutrients

FARMER WITH CHICKENS IN THE BARNYARD
Coastal Ridge, Santa Clara County

APRICOT ORCHARD
Santa Clara Valley

than non-organic soil. This is because non-organic farmers usually fertilize their soil with only three components: nitrogen, phosphorus and potassium, whereas organic farmers use a variety of natural materials and methods to fertilize their soil, including compost, manure and cover crops. And what's not in the soil cannot be absorbed by the plant. So when we buy organic produce we not only get chemical-free food, but we also get all the health benefits that rich, well-managed soil provides.

One more way organic foods are better for our health is that organic producers are not allowed to use any Genetically Modified Organisms or GMOs at any level of their production. This relatively new technology is little understood and inadequately tested to insure consumer safety. GMO technology inserts genes from one species into another, in an attempt to transfer certain desired traits. For example, the Flavr-Savr tomato was created when scientists inserted cold water fish genes into tomatoes to make them more frost-resistant and to give them a longer shelf-life. The consequences of crossing species barriers like this, which is impossible in nature, are unknown, as are the risks to human health and the environment. However, more than 70% of all non-organic foods in the U.S. already contain GMOs. So, the only way to limit our exposure to GMOs is by purchasing local and organic foods whenever possible.

Why Sustainable?

The foundation of organic agriculture is building and maintaining excellent soil. Plants grown on healthy soil are less susceptible to pests and the need for pest eradication is reduced. Chemical-based agriculture however, begins with soil which is already nutrient depleted. Plants grown on depleted soil are weaker and more prone to disease and pests, so more chemicals are needed every year. The farmer gets caught in a vicious downward spiral by becoming more and more dependent on harmful chemicals, eventually ending up with sterile and depleted soil and chemical-resistant pests. On the other hand, when pests become a problem on organic farms, growers use Integrated Pest Management methods, which actually enhance the overall biodiversity and health of the ecosystem by introducing beneficial plants and insects that restore nature's balance. Furthermore, organic farming not only protects the soil but other resources as well, such as water. Rich organic topsoil has a great water-holding capacity so less water is needed for irrigation. In addition, by not using harmful chemicals on the farm, waterways, rivers and streams are kept cleaner.

Systems which integrate the environment, the economy, and social concerns in a way that can be maintained in a healthy state indefinitely can be defined as sustainable. Therefore, sustainable agriculture must be economically viable, socially responsible, and ecologically sound. In terms of food production, sustainable agriculture cannot use up resources—soil, water, labor, community support, etc.—faster than it can replenish them. On the other hand, any type of agriculture that uses up or degrades its natural resource base, or pollutes the environment, will, over time, lose its ability to be productive. At the same time, agriculture that isn't profitable will drive farmers out of business. What this means is that agriculture that fails to meet the needs of both the environment and society cannot be sustained. So, look for the local and organic label at retail outlets and farmers' markets in your area. Present and future generations will thank you for it.

–Helge Hellberg

Helge Hellberg is the Executive Director of *Marin Organic*, promoting and supporting local organic agriculture by creating partnerships and alliances among educational and environmental organizations, food producers, consumers and retailers. Hellberg is currently working on a book that takes an in-depth look at the benefits of local and organic agriculture. To learn more about *Marin Organic* please go to www.marin-organic.org.

Scenes at the farmers market in Point Reyes

HARRIS RANCH
Off Highway 5 and Highway 41
Harris Ranch is the biggest
cattle operation in California.

FARMS BIG AND SMALL...

For the past 50 years California farmers have led the nation in agricultural production. The latest figures put their cash earnings at about $27 billion annually, which makes agriculture California's most important industry. About a third of the state's land is devoted to farmland. The Central Valley accounts for almost half of the farmland, two-thirds of the cropland, and almost 75 percent of the irrigated land. Valley farmland is threatened by a population explosion that is expected to grow by 24 percent before 2010.

Driving through the valley, one is struck by how huge the farms seem, yet the California Farm Bureau boasts that the average California farm is smaller than the national average. They state that 97 percent of farms are family-owned or partnerships, but if you look closely at their figures you discover that almost 83 percent of the land is owned by 20 percent of the farmers. Maybe it is true that many of these are "family" corporations but they are a long way from forty acres and a plow.

ROUGE ET NOIR BRIE
Marin French Cheese Company

TOMALES FARM
A small grass-fed beef ranch.

Bull in Snow

Cow on the Edge of Fog
Sonoma County

Cow Sticking Its Tongue Out

Cow Contemplating The Void
Nicasio

Udder Confusion
Straus Farm

COWS, TOMALES BAY, AND SONOMA HILLS
Point Reyes National Seashore

STRAUS ORGANIC MILK

Who doesn't like ice cream or a glass of cold milk with chocolate cake? And we confess to liking a steak every now and then. In West Marin, where we live, cows are the main farm animal, taking advantage of this area's natural grasslands and gently rolling hills.

Those who farm in West Marin must be creative and nimble to survive the challenges of modern agriculture. The massive livestock operations of the Central Valley enjoy a competitive edge from huge economies of scale, forcing family farms to seek other ways to survive. A prime example is the Straus Family Creamery of West Marin, a pioneer in producing organic milk and cream sold throughout California.

DOMESTIC TURKEYS
Rural Marin

259

Square Hay Bales
Marin-Sonoma Border

Windmill and Water Tank
Highway 25, near Pinnacles

Aeromotor Blades

FARM WITH SHEEP
Coastal Range Behind Big Sur

HARVESTING ASPARAGUS BY HAND
Central Valley

FARM WORKERS WITH BROCCOLI
Santa Maria

It is a humbling experience to see how hard the farm workers toil in the fields of California. The conditions are normally hot and dusty; the dust is often contaminated with fertilizers and pesticides. There is a certain brutality in being paid piecemeal. Your worth depends on how many vegetables or fruits you pick rather than how many hours you work or the quality of your labor.

Major improvements in working conditions of the farm workers were brought about in the 1960s with the successes of the United Farm Workers Union, led by Cesar Chavez. The union organized strikes in the fields and consumer boycotts of products like lettuce from Salinas and grapes from Delano. They set up picket lines at Safeway's and reminded consumers that their food did not magically appear from heaven and drop into supermarket shelves, packaged for their convenience, but arrived as a result of gruelling labor.

UFW Picketing Safeway
Berkeley

Farmers and agricultural scientists deserve much of the credit for California's bounty, but we would not be enjoying it without the farm workers, many of whom undergo incredible hardship to get into America and do this hard work. They deserve all the support we can give them.

Farm Workers at End of Day
Santa Maria

Farm Produce
Market, San Francisco

Laotian Family Farm
Sacramento Delta

Laotian Strawberry Salesman

MOONRISE AT RESPINI RANCH
Marshall

BARN IN THE MIST
Gale Livestock, Marin County
This ranch sells grass-fed beef and is becoming organic certified.

Chapter 17

Earthquakes and Fires

California shakes and bakes.

AFTERMATH OF THE 1989 EARTHQUAKE

SAN FRANCISCO PIER FIRE

THE COLLAPSE OF THE NIMITZ FREEWAY, INTERSTATE 880, IN OAKLAND
Forty-two people died because of the failure of this viaduct.

One cannot even begin to consider oneself a Californian until one has been through at least one significant earthquake. The first one I felt was in the late 1970s in downtown San Francisco. I was working on the 30th floor of a building when I looked outside and noticed the men working on the construction of the high-rise next to ours were swaying. Then I felt it myself. I had a mat knife in my hand and my first thought was to get rid of that so I wouldn't stab myself. Someone announced we should leave the building and we all calmly walked down 30 flights of stairs. Along with hundreds of others, we waited on the street for 30 minutes and then returned to work.

The next major earthquake I felt was in 1989 when the Bay Bridge collapsed. At the time we had an photography studio in Berkeley and Richard was photographing a pyramid of cans of stewed tomatoes. The art director was agonizing over whether a few fresh cherry tomatoes at the bottom of the pyramid would distract the viewer from the cans. It was driving Richard crazy. It was almost five o' clock and he still hadn't shot a sheet of film. Sometimes, even if you are getting paid well by the hour, enough is enough. Richard said to the client, "There's going to be a big earthquake, the lights are going to go out and all the cans will fall down. Why don't I shoot it now, with and without the tomatoes?" The client looked at him as if he were insane, but agreed. Richard shot the set-up every which way and then retired to the bathroom to read the newspaper. The art director continued to fuss. The next minute the toilet bowl started to sway. The bathroom was well constructed, so Richard thought it would be the safest place

The San Francisco-Oakland Bay Bridge With A Coast Guard Vessel
San Francisco Bay

to stay. He shouted to the client to get under a doorway. After it was over, everything was as he had predicted—no power, the 12-foot-high mono-pod and camera had jumped six feet and the cans were all over the floor. The client was screaming and looking at Richard as if he were the devil. She ran out of the studio never to be seen there again! "I thought she would be happy that I predicted the earthquake and got the shot, but I think somehow she thought I was to blame for it," Richard said ruefully.

Meanwhile, I had gone to the southernmost part of nearby Alameda to deliver a job. As I drove back toward the freeway I heard an announcement on the radio that there had been a toxic spill on the route I had planned to take, the Nimitz Freeway. I decided to drive back to Berkeley using city streets. I drove about ten miles on East 14th Street, something I had never done before. As a result, I was well away from the Cypress Overpass when it collapsed. During the earthquake, I lost control of my car and thought I had a flat tire until I noticed all the telephone poles were swaying. The strange thing is that I was later unable to trace the source of the radio announcement I had heard. Some things in life are inexplicable.

After the earthquake, I made my way back to the studio. We then picked up Richard's mother, who understandably was quite agitated. We heard that the Bay Bridge had collapsed and decided to go out in our sailboat to see if we could rescue anyone. We didn't find anyone in need, but we took some unusual pictures of the bridge.

–Kathleen Goodwin

Bay Bridge Collapse Detail

FIRE IN THE OAKLAND HILLS

OAKLAND HILLS FIRE, 1991

The house in the foreground of this picture was lost in the fire and this photo was used by the architect to recreate it. The day of the Berkeley-Oakland Hills fire Richard was in Alameda tying to sell a camera at a swap meet. He was unsuccessful and on his way home he saw the hills on fire. He drove up to see and to help if possible. He had only two frames left in the camera and took this photograph. Nearby he found a dazed man with Alzheimer's and got him a ride to safety.

HILLER HIGHLANDS
Berkeley-Oakland Hills Fire
The fire ultimately killed 25 people and injured 150 others. The 1,520 acres destroyed included 2,449 single-family dwellings and 437 apartments.

TREE FORMS
Berkeley-Oakland Hills Fire

SWIMMING POOL
Berkeley-Oakland Hills Fire

TENNIS IN THE FIRE AREA
Berkeley-Oakland Hills Fire

Fires move in mysterious ways. The Chabot tennis courts survived the Berkeley-Oakland fire while all around them houses burned to the ground. Perhaps this picture is symbolic of the ability of Californians to enjoy their lives despite the turmoil around them—or are they just wearing blinders and going on blithely?

The Horse Stables at Yosemite National Park Burning, 1971
Yosemite National Park

Firemen Working on the Fire
Yosemite National Park

Mount Vision Fire at Sunset
Tomales Bay

WILD FIRES

Mount Vision Fire at Night, 1995
Point Reyes
A massive wildfire that started on Mount Vision in the
Point Reyes National Seashore burned thousands of
acres of parkland and consumed 40 homes.

Chapter 18

Green California

Green is the prime color of the world, and that from which its loveliness arises.

–Pedro Calderon De La Barca, 17th Century Spanish Poet

WINDMILLS, OLD AND NEW
Altamont

RECYCLING
Port of Redwood City

Rows of windmills covering hills. Bicycles carried on the backs of buses. Solar panels on urban houses. Green mulch and blue recycling bins lining suburban streets. All results of the Green Movement. Small steps, but positive, and multiplied globally, a powerful effect.

I have a personal vendetta against invasive thistles and have cleared trails where I live of their thorny presence. After diligently returning each spring for five years, I have cleared the hillside—for a while at least. A small victory.

Many Californians have embraced a green way of life: recycling, fuel-efficient, low-emission vehicles, solar energy, appreciation of the natural landscape, carpooling. However, supplying its residents (more than 33 million) with healthy food and pure water, plus dealing with the waste stream they generate, is a major challenge.

The state's huge industrial and agricultural economic base means the potential for environmental degradation is correspondingly on a giant scale. Add corrupt politicians and bureaucrats, add oil company lobbying and the politics of water, and California is truly threatened.

The state was developed when automobiles were king, which led to massive air pollution and an unwieldy proliferation of roads. Wiser sentiments are now beginning to take control. Carpooling lanes are the norm on city highways, and buses, subway, and light rail systems, along with bicycle usage, are growing. The quality of the air is actually improving.

Organic farming is making inroads into the disastrous overuse of pesticides that has poisoned farm workers, drinking-water sources and

the flora and fauna. If we compare San Francisco Bay today with the ecological paradise that the first Europeans found, with whales in the bay, huge salmon runs, abundant wildlife and shellfish, it would seem like the biological health of our region is perhaps a hundredth of what it was before, and the remaining birds and animals just tiny groups of survivors. Other areas of the state, like the Trinity Mountains to the north and the Coast Range, are closer to the original wildness and diversity. While the grizzly bear is gone, one can still get some idea in those areas of what primal California must have been like.

What will the state look like in 100 years? Will it be one big suburb, with desalination plants, powered by nuclear power, pumping out water from the ocean? Can we kick our fossil fuel habit before the effects of global warming are irreversible?

Imagine California with idyllic valleys and sustainable farming, cute little towns, fresh air, organic crops, good public transportation, non-polluting industries and electric cars. Imagine everyone doing their part to make California clean, peaceful and sane.

It all begins with the people in our democracy: voting for green-thinking candidates, living cleanly, sharing rather than duplicating resources, keeping the family size small, learning to cooperate for our needs—all of these actions will contribute to a healthier world.

Americans now drive in isolation, watch TV in isolation and seem to have lost the feeling of community that was a bigger part of their lives in the past. A model of California with people living in a nice neighborhood trying to help each other and have fun together isn't such a bad idea, but it sure is hard to turn this "shop-till-you-drop" culture into a more nature-loving, hang-out kind of scene.

Do you think that the billionaires of the world—Bill Gates and friends—enjoy life so much more than middle-class people? If you have love, friends, and interesting work, don't bet on it.

The images in this chapter, photographed over many years, document green practices as well as graphic scenes of pollution in highly degraded landscapes. We hope our pictures will influence you to think of your highly stressed Mother Earth when you go about your life and make your choices. Here is a summary of the challenges we all face. It is inspired by the Sierra Club's website.

SPRAWL

The costs and consequences of poorly planned development have become clear; Americans want better, smarter ways to grow.

WILDLANDS CAMPAIGN

America was once a vast expanse of unbroken wilderness. We should secure lasting protection for the 100 million acres of habitat remaining.

FOREST PROTECTION & RESTORATION

Teddy Roosevelt established the National Forests more than 100 years ago. Today they are a patchwork of clear-cuts and logging roads.

CLEAN WATER

America's water is threatened by pollution, wetland destruction, and factory farms—some of the nation's most virulent pollluters.

GLOBAL WARMING

Rising levels of carbon dioxide can doom the planet's living systems.

HUMAN RIGHTS & THE ENVIRONMENT

Around the world, environmentalists fighting pollution and irresponsible development are often persecuted for their efforts to protect the Earth.

GLOBAL POPULATION

Family planning ensures healthy families and a healthy environment.

RESPONSIBLE TRADE

Free trade can be transformed into responsible trade, protecting our rich natural heritage and our children's future.

CLEAN AIR

Nationwide, high smog levels cause 159,000 trips to emergency rooms, 53,000 hospital admissions, and 6 million asthma attacks each summer.

CORPORATE ACCOUNTABILITY

Corporate abuse of power interferes with the ability of communities and nations to protect the environment.

ENVIRONMENTAL EDUCATION

We must make sure that our kids are taught about how people affect the planet and what we can do to create a sustainable future.

ENVIRONMENTAL JUSTICE

Impoverished areas and countries should not be the dumping ground for polluting industries and toxics.

FACTORY FARMS

Giant livestock operations are a growing public health threat all across the nation. These corporate-controlled units—where tens of thousands of animals are "produced" in factory-like settings—are polluting our water and air.

GENETIC ENGINEERING

Full public disclosure, discussion, and evaluation of the potential hazards and benefits of genetic engineering are needed.

GRAZING

Livestock production on our public lands is having negative effects on wildlife in the Western states.

MARINE WILDLIFE AND HABITAT

Our oceans harbor a rich diversity of habitats and species. Yet almost no area of the ocean is off-limits to human use and abuse, including extraction of living and non-living resources, pollution, and habitat destruction.

SPECIES AND HABITAT

We must strengthen protections for endangered species, enforce our environmental laws, and end destructive land use practices.

NUCLEAR WASTE

Nuclear waste accumulation is accelerating, and no reasonable plan for its permanent isolation has been developed anywhere in the world.

RECREATION ISSUES

Keep parks clean and help maintain them by being a volunteer. Please vote for more natural recreation areas.

SUSTAINABLE CONSUMPTION

Buy, make, build using products and services with an eye toward the environment.

TOXICS

Toxic chemical pollution threatens every American family and every community.

TRASH TRANSFER

Trash transfer stations threaten neighbors' health, property values, and quality of life.

TRANSPORTATION

Transportation choices, such as rail, buses, and bikes, help reduce air and water pollution, save energy, protect open space, reduce traffic, and enhance the livability of our communities.

WETLANDS

Wetlands filter pollutants from our air and drinking water, protect our homes by storing floodwater, and absorb water-borne pollutants and contaminants.

WILDLIFE

Learn about the creatures with whom we share the planet; protect them and their habitats.

SNOWY EGRET
Lake Merritt

WILD ANIMALS HAVING A BAD HUMAN DAY

SEAGULL WITH FISH HOOK AND LINE

WILD BURRO EATING DONUTS

OIL WELL, CENTRAL VALLEY

TOXIC WASTE BARRELS

CHEVRON REFINERY, RICHMOND

ENERGY USAGE AND GLOBAL WARMING
We all have to relearn our three Rs — Reduce, Reuse, Recycle!

Society-wide planning could get some of us out of cars through efficient, intercity high-speed trains. A high-speed rail system is on the drawing board to connect Los Angeles with San Francisco. Environmentalists are supporting it, with the proviso that every station have an urban growth boundary so that the new system does not encourage urban sprawl. We hope more cars will be electric in the future so we could greatly reduce greenhouse gas emissions. In the meantime, hybrid cars are a very positive step, but regular, gas-powered vehicles can be made far more fuel efficient right now. When solar panels are on millions of roofs, the need for power plants will be greatly reduced. Wind energy is practical in certain places if done right. A healthy attitude toward energy use is helpful, for example, "The less energy you use, the more energy you'll have." Why do some people need those giant cars and trucks (off-road bad boys)? When a friend of mine sees the trucks with the big tires, he says, "The bigger the tires, the smaller the penis!"

COVER THE EARTH, EMERYVILLE, 1971

LOGGING, SIERRA

FARMLAND TO SUBURBIA

SUBURBIA NEAR S.F. AIRPORT

SHASTA LAKE HOUSEBOATS

SHOPPING MALL

GOING SHOPPING

NUKES IN CALIFORNIA?

The ultimate un-ecological activity is nuclear war. This Nike missile on Mt. Tam had a nuclear warhead. It was designed to kill Russian bombers off the California coast with a mushroom cloud, which could have drifted back to San Francisco. The submarine, photographed as it made its way up to Mare Island, could have been armed with nuclear missiles.

California is an oddity in so many ways. It is the state that leads in recycling, buying hybrid cars—in many ways it's the greenest state. But the flip side is California's *military-industrial complex*, first warned of by Dwight Eisenhower, who, as Commander-in-Chief in World War II fighting the Nazis and Fascism, saw the tragic effects of wars. He had no romantic fantasy about the glory of war. He foresaw the growth of giant military contractors, such as Lockheed. These companies, founded to profit from the making of military equipment and developing increas-

Nike Missile on Mt. Tamalpais—now an exhibit

Greenpeace: The Rainbow Warrior
Anti-nuke ship later blown up by the French Secret Service.

ingly powerful weapons, are a huge part of the California economy. They could, through political might, actually influence the use of those products to put the nation in a permanent war state—or have they already?

President Bush has used the terrorist attack on America to attack Iraq on the false pretense of their possession of weapons of mass destruction, furthering the fortunes of these companies.

Author Mike Davis called the stealth bombers being built in the California desert "hot rods of the apocalypse."

California leads the nation in the design and production of weapons of mass destruction.

Submarine Under the Richmond Bridge

Lawrence Livermore Lab's Computer Room
California's Leading Nuclear Design Facility

Some solutions to California's environmental challenges are shown here.

Bay Area Rapid Transit (BART)

Solar Panels

Bird-Safe Windmills (no guy-lines, larger, slower blades)

Toxic Day
Point Reyes
Many counties hold toxic days, when local residents can bring toxic household waste to be disposed of responsibly. Unused paint and unwanted household chemicals can find new homes, or be disposed of safely.

Biking

Richard Blair and Kathleen Goodwin at the studio (and Eshowe, the dog)

Fog in the morning from the studio

Blair-Goodwin Gallery

Interior View

Quail on the studio deck

AUTHORS' COMMENTS

This book is a pioneering project in book publishing. We call it an artisan book because we took the photographs, wrote the text, scanned the images, and designed the book as a combined process. Except for running the press and the bindery work, we did it all. Owning the computer and scanning equipment, we were totally free to do what we wanted, without a client, deadline, or publisher. Knowing the entire process allowed a rare degree of creative freedom and a tight integration of all the aspects of publishing the book, including marketing. While Kathleen and Richard were co-authors and Richard was the principal photographer and book designer, we collaborated to the point of exhausted harmony, with both of us working on everything together. We are both everywhere in the book. We lugged cameras and scurried when the light was happening. Anecdotes slowly became facts. Learning computer programs, keeping the computers running, and archiving the work were Herculean tasks. Every step had obstacles. We worked when we had the confidence to proceed. The payoff came when we could visualize and create fearlessly. We hope you enjoy this book as much as we enjoyed creating it.

ACKNOWLEDGMENTS

We want to thank Nancy Adess, who edited the book with humor and forbearance. She raised the level of our writing, and our honesty! Michael Taylor, a gifted author, was our rewrite man. He took the prose and reworked it where necessary. He did his best, but the final responsibility is ours. Marcus Hanschen, formerly a talented staff photographer for our photography studio, gave us invaluable advice. John Herbert helped with the photo research. Rima Blair encouraged us to finish the book. *Life* photographer Dennis Stock's book, *California Trip*, 1970, inspired Richard, but the books are unrelated. Our late parents, Ponty and Malcolm Goodwin and Ann and Hugh E. Blair, were uniquely talented and skilled in ways that provided the foundation we needed to publish this work. *"Teach your children well,"* as the song says.

ORDERING PHOTOGRAPHS AND BOOKS

All the images in the book are available as fine art prints. Prices depend on the size of the image, the edition, and the print process used: archival black & white, or pigment prints. We print images in the darkroom or with archival papers that last at least 100 years. Our catalog of photographs is on the web at BlairGoodwinGallery.com. You can also contact our office at 415 663-1615 for print and book orders. Books are available directly from us (signed!) via the web, or your local bookstore may have them in stock or can order them for you.

BLAIR GOODWIN GALLERY

Open studio events are a wonderful way to see artists in their work environment and support their work. We host open studios where we show the public our artwork and sell images both humble and grand. Kind words of encouragement are all that's needed for a visit, but you may fall in love with a piece. We present slide shows and discussions on photography and current issues. Write or call us for studio event information. Or sign up for our e-mail list at our website.

WORKSHOPS AND CLASSES

We teach classes in photography and publication arts. The workshops, held in West Marin, combine learning with the experience of our incredible environment. They include landscape work at national parks, as well as classes in book publishing at our studio atop Inverness Ridge. The skills needed to turn writing, painting and photography into books are taught. Please check the website for class information or e-mail rk@pointreyesvisions.com to be put on the mailing list.

OTHER BOOKS BY GOODWIN AND BLAIR

Point Reyes Visions (cloth & paperback)
Point Reyes Visions Guidebook (cloth & paper)
Published by Color & Light Editions,
Available from the publisher.
The Great Potato Book
Firecrackers-The Art & History
Published by Ten Speed Press, Berkeley.
San Francisco, Sights and Secrets
Published by Chronicle Books, S.F.
(major contributor, both editions)

Color & Light Editions
PO Box 934
Inverness, CA 94937
415-663-1615
BlairGoodwinGallery.com
email: rk@pointreyesvisions.com

We wish to thank the following people at Craft Print International Ltd., who printed this book: Charlie Chan, *Managing Director*, Desmond Chan and Joyce Ng. Prepress: Wong Chew Choon and staff. Printers: Leong Yuen Sang, Tan Chew Hee, Tan Joo Teck, Loh Siew Loon, Jackson Lee Thiam Ting and Xie Hai Feng.

ELEPHANT MOUNTAIN SUNSET
Point Reyes
KATHLEEN GOODWIN

Color & Light Editions

PO Box 934

Inverness, CA 94937

415-663-1615

BlairGoodwinGallery.com